Third Edition

SPANISH VERB DRILLS

by
Vivienne Bey

in collaboration with
Beatrice Concheff

Mc
Graw
Hill

New York   Chicago   San Francisco   Lisbon   London   Madrid   Mexico City
Milan   New Delhi   San Juan   Seoul   Singapore   Sydney   Toronto

9 10 11 12 13 14 15 16 17 18 19 20 21 22 23 24 25   CUS/CUS   0 9

ISBN-13: 978-0-07-142090-7
ISBN-10:   0-07-142090-8
Library of Congress Control Number: 2004268083

McGraw-Hill books are available at special quantity discounts to use as premiums and sales
promotions, or for use in corporate training programs. For more information, please write to
the Director of Special Sales, Professional Publishing, McGraw-Hill, Two Penn Plaza, New
York, NY 10121-2298. Or contact your local bookstore.

This book is printed on acid-free paper.

Contents

Introduction

Spanish Verb Drills is designed to help learners develop mastery of the Spanish verb system. Created to supplement the oral and written verb practice offered by standard Spanish-language textbooks, it provides students at all levels with the drill and review needed to grasp the tenses and conjugations of Spanish verbs.

Models at the beginning of each unit establish the patterns to be reinforced in the *Para practicar* drills, the *Aplicación* exercises, and the Mastery Tests. In addition, the four-part *Repaso general* allows students to test themselves for overall control of the Spanish verb system.

Combining the features of a workbook, textbook, and self-study manual, *Spanish Verb Drills* clearly and systematically explains the workings of the Spanish verb system, while providing numerous and varied exercises for thorough practice of each point covered. In addition, the Answer Key at the back of this edition provides valuable support when learners need to clarify a concept immediately.

Covering verb tenses ranging from the present indicative to the imperfect subjunctive and offering detailed treatment of stem-changing verbs, orthographic-changing verbs, and irregular verbs, *Spanish Verb Drills* will serve as an important study aid to all those wishing to perfect their knowledge of Spanish verbs. Equally suitable in a Spanish-language course or for self-study, this book effectively clarifies the complexities of this crucial area of Spanish-language study.

Regular Verbs
Present

Spanish verbs are classified into three classes, or *conjugations*, according to the final letters of their infinitives. The present tense of regular verbs is formed by adding the personal endings to the *stem*, which is determined by dropping the *-ar*, *-er*, or *-ir* of the infinitive.

	1	*2*	*3*
	*habl*ar to speak	*com*er to eat	*part*ir to leave
yo	habl *o* I speak, am speaking, do speak	com *o* I eat, etc.	part *o* I leave, etc.
tú	habl *as* you speak, etc.	com *es* you eat, etc.	part *es* you leave, etc.
Ud.	habl *a* you speak, etc.	com *e* you eat, etc.	part *e* you leave, etc.
él(ella)	habl *a* he(she) speaks, etc.	com *e* he(she) eats, etc.	part *e* he(she) leaves, etc.
nosotros	habl *amos* we speak, etc.	com *emos* we eat, etc.	part *imos* we leave, etc.
vosotros	habl *áis* you speak, etc.	com *éis* you eat, etc.	part *ís* you leave, etc.
Uds.	habl *an* you speak, etc.	com *en* you eat, etc.	part *en* you leave, etc.
ellos (ellas)	habl *an* they speak, etc.	com *en* they eat, etc.	part *en* they leave, etc.

1. Spanish has no equivalent for the English *am* (is, are) or *do* (does) in the present tense. The single verb *hablo* means *I am speaking*, *I do speak*, or *I speak*.

2. The pronoun subject of the Spanish verb is expressed by the ending of the verb. The verb must show this personal ending, even if a subject pronoun or noun is already present in the sentence. The subject pronouns (*yo*, etc.) are seldom used in actual practice, except for *Ud.* and *Uds.* Remember that there are two singular and two plural forms of the second person (you), for informal and formal use. The *tú* and *vosotros* forms of the verb may not be used with the subjects *Ud.* and *Uds.*, or vice versa.

Negative: All Spanish verbs form the negative by placing *no* before the verb.

He eats *come*;   he does not eat *no come*.

Interrogative: All Spanish verbs in the interrogative are identical to the affirmative.

He eats *come*;   does he eat? *¿come?*

Spanish verbs in the negative-interrogative are identical to the negative.

He does not eat *no come*;   doesn't he eat? *¿no come?*

Para practicar

All regular verbs with infinitives ending in *-ar* form the present like *hablar*. Write the present tense of (1) *acabar* to finish, and (2) *tomar* to take.

(1) **acabar** yo *Acabo*

tú *Acabas*

Ud. *Acaba*

él *Acaba*

nosotros *Acabamos*

vosotros

Uds. *Acaban*

ellos *Acaban*

(2) **tomar** yo *Tomo*

tú *Tomas*

Ud. *Toma*

ella *Toma*

nosotros *Tomemos*

vosotros

Uds. *Toman*

ellos *Toman*

All regular verbs with infinitives in *-er* form the present like *comer*. Write the present tense of (1) *vender* to sell, and (2) *beber* to drink.

(1) **vender** yo *Vendo*

tú *Vendes*

Ud. *Vende*

él *Vende*

nosotros *Vendemos*

vosotros

Uds. *Venden*

ellos *Venden*

(2) **beber** yo *Bebo*

tú *bebes*

Ud. *bebe*

él *bebe*

nosotros *bebemos*

vosotros

Uds. *Beben*

ellos *Beben*

All regular verbs with infinitives in *-ir* form the present like *partir*. Write the present tense of (1) *vivir* to live, and (2) *recibir* to receive.

(1) **vivir** yo _vivo_

tú _vives_

Ud. _vive_

él _vive_

nosotros _vivimos_

vosotros _____

Uds. _viven_

ellos _viven_

(2) **recibir** yo _recibo_

tú _recibes_

Ud. _recibe_

él _recibe_

nosotros _recibimos_

vosotros _____

Uds. _reciben_

ellos _reciben_

Change the infinitives below into the correct form of the present, according to the subject indicated:

yo

estudiar _Estudio_   comprender _comprendo_   temer _Temo_   necesitar _necesito_   partir _parto_   enseñar _Enseño_

vender _vendo_

tú

hablar _Hablas_   asistir _Asistes_   abrir _Abres_   beber _bebes_   preguntar _Preguntas_   tomar _Tomas_

escuchar _Escuchas_

Ud.

contestar	abrir	aprender	entrar	leer	vivir
Contesta	*Abre*	*Aprende*	*Entra*	*Le*	*Vive*

comer
Come

Juan (what person?)

escribir	estudiar	acabar	temer	partir	comprender
Escribe	*Estudia*	*Acaba*	*Teme*	*parte*	*Comprende*

vender
vende

nosotros

aprender	asistir	tomar	escuchar	hablar	vivir
aprendemos	*Asistimos*	*Tomemos*	*Escuchemos*	*Hablemos*	*vivimos*

temer
Tememos

vosotros

hablar	asistir	beber	leer	tomar	llevar
Habla					

enseñar

Uds.

comer	escribir	necesitar	entrar	acabar	leer
Comen	*Escriben*	*Necesitan*	*Entran*	*Acaban*	*Lean*

vivir
viven

María y Juan (what person?)

temer	llevar	estudiar	preguntar	contestar	comprender
Temen	*llevan*	*Estudian*	*Preguntan*	*Contestan*	*Comprenden*

partir

parten

Aplicación

A. Write the verb forms in the person indicated by the pronoun:

1. nosotros (tomar) *Tomamos*
2. él (aprender) *Aprende*
3. ellos (vender) *venden*
4. yo (asistir) *Asisto*
5. tú (contestar) *Contestas*
6. Ud. (beber) *bebe*
7. nosotras (abrir) *Abrimos*
8. ella (necesitar) *necesita*
9. vosotros (tomar) _____
10. ella (leer) *Lee*
11. yo (aprender) *Aprendo*
12. nosotros (temer) *Tememos*
13. vosotros (recibir) _____

14. ellos (escribir) *Escriben*
15. ella (abrir) *Abre*
16. nosotros (enseñar) *Enseñamos*
17. yo (contestar) *Contesto*
18. nosotros (estudiar) *Estudiamos*
19. yo (abrir) *Abro*
20. ella (tomar) *Toma*
21. Ud. (preguntar) *pregunta*
22. ellas (leer) *Leen*
23. ellos (recibir) *Reciben*
24. tú (temer) *Temes*
25. nosotras (leer) *Leemos*

B. Change each verb form to the corresponding person of the plural, and translate the plural verb into English:

1. escribo *I write*

2. él contesta *He protest*
   He answer

3. vivo *I live*

4. Ud. necesita *necesita*

5. él bebe *He drinks*

6. aprendes *You learn*

7. él vende *He sells*

8. asisto *I attend*

9. Ud. enseña *You teach*

10. abres

11. Ud. comprende

12. ella escucha

13. temes *You fear*

14. ella pregunta *She question*

15. Ud. lee *you read*

16. tomo *I drink*

17. recibo *I receive*

18. él estudia

19. necesito

20. escribes

Mastery Test

estudiar to study	*trabajar* to work	esconder to hide
necesitar to need	*comprender* to understand	*vivir* to live
contestar to answer	*beber* to drink	*recibir* to receive
preguntar to ask	*vender* to sell	*asistir* to attend
enseñar to teach	*aprender* to learn	*abrir* to open
escuchar to listen	*temer* to fear	*escribir* to write
tomar to take	*leer* to read	*unir* to join, unite
entrar to enter	*creer* to believe	

Translate the following, using the above list of infinitives:

1. we answer

2. you (pl., fam.) sell

3. he is asking

4. they do sell

5. we do not need _____

6. we study _____

7. I am learning _____

8. do they listen? _____

9. he is not reading _____

10. you (s., for.) are not entering _____

11. we work _____

12. do you write? _____

13. they do ask _____

14. you (pl., for.) are taking _____

15. I sell _____

16. she does not work _____

17. they do not believe _____

18. they hide _____

19. he writes _____

20. do you fear? _____

21. we are living _____

22. he teaches _____

23. she fears _____

24. you (pl., fam.) receive _____

25. he is opening _____

26. they do not take _____

27. we attend _____

28. is he selling? _____

29. I study _____

30. I believe _____ _____

31. they unite _____

32. they are not opening _____

33. you teach _____

34. he attends _____

35. we ask _____

36. do you (pl., for.) learn? _____

37. she drinks _____

38. are you (s., fam.) studying? _____

39. you (s., for.) live _____

40. they enter _____

Imperfect

The imperfect is formed by adding the appropriate endings to the stem.

	1	*2*	*3*
	hablar	**comer**	**partir**
yo	habl *aba* I was speaking,	com *ía* I was eating,	part *ía* I was leaving,
tú	habl *abas* used to speak	com *ías* used to eat	part *ías* used to leave
Ud.	habl *aba*	com *ía*	part *ía*
él(ella)	habl *aba*	com *ía*	part *ía*
nosotros	habl *ábamos*	com *íamos*	part *íamos*
vosotros	habl *abais*	com *íais*	part *íais*
Uds.	habl *aban*	com *ían*	part *ían*
ellos	habl *aban*	com *ían*	part *ían*

Note: The imperfect is translated as *I spoke* or *I did speak* in actual practice as well as the meanings given above. For drill purposes, however, this manual will consider *I was speaking* or *I used to speak* (*you*, *he*, etc.) as translations of the imperfect. Interrogative imperfect is *was I speaking* or *did I speak* and negative imperfect is *I was not speaking* or *I did not speak*.

All forms of the imperfect of *-er* and *-ir* verbs must have a written accent. Because first- and third-person singular forms are identical, context determines the subject for them.

Para practicar

Write the form of the imperfect that corresponds to the subject indicated:

yo

tomar	meter	vivir	comprar	sentir	viajar
——————	——————	——————	——————	——————	——————

correr

——————

tú

aprender	subir	pasar	guardar	coser	esperar
——————	——————	——————	——————	——————	——————

acabar

——————

Ud.

tocar	amar	saber	jugar	viajar	comprender
_____	_____	_____	_____	_____	_____

escribir

_____

María

echar	preparar	leer	vivir	abrir	correr
_____	_____	_____	_____	_____	_____

trabajar

_____

nosotros

estudiar	vender	subir	comprender	abrir	preparar
_____	_____	_____	_____	_____	_____

tomar

_____

vosotros

escribir	trabajar	comer	beber	recibir	comprar
_____	_____	_____	_____	_____	_____

llevar

_____

Juan y Ud. (What person?)

pasar	caminar	responder	subir	hablar	abrir
_____	_____	_____	_____	_____	_____

sacar

_____

ellos

acabar	salir	contestar	vivir	guardar	correr
_____	_____	_____	_____	_____	_____

viajar

_____

Aplicación

A. Write the imperfect form in the person indicated by the subject:

1. él (hablar) _____

2. Elena y yo (vivir) _____

3. ella (saber) _____

4. Uds. (conocer) _____

5. los niños (pedir) _____

6. nosotros (correr) _____

7. tú (partir) _____

8. yo (pasar) _____

9. vosotros (esperar) _____

10. Uds. (acabar) _____

11. Ud. (caminar) _____

12. él (comprender) _____

13. Juan y Pedro (tomar) _____

14. yo (escribir) _____

15. Ud. (amar) _____

16. vosotros (conocer) _____

B. Change to imperfect and translate new form into English:

1. contestamos _____

2. vendes _____

3. él pregunta _____

4. aprendo _____

5. ellos escuchan _____

6. Ud. escribe _____

7. ellos aprenden _____

8. Ud. estudia _____

9. vivimos _____

10. él teme _____

11. él abre _____

12. ellos enseñan _____

13. él asiste _____

14. tomamos _____

15. leo _____

16. Uds. beben _____

17. tú (beber) _____

18. nosotros (comprar) _____

19. ellos (subir) _____

20. yo (correr) _____

21. ella (responder) _____

22. tú (guardar) _____

23. Ud. (aprender) _____

24. Juan y él (llevar) _____

25. vosotros (pasar) _____

17. temo _____

18. ellos reciben _____

19. necesito _____

20. Uds. viven _____

21. abrimos _____

22. contestáis _____

23. tomas _____

24. él bebe _____

25. abrís _____

Mastery Test

Write the Spanish that corresponds to the English verb forms, selecting the correct verb from the list on page 6.

1. they used to live _____

2. we were working _____

3. you (s., fam.) were not selling _____

_____

4. we used to live _____

5. they did not need _____

6. you (s., for.) were learning _____

_____

7. he used to believe _____

8. you (pl., fam.) were asking _____

_____

9. I used to fear _____

10. did you (s., fam.) understand? _____

_____

11. she was teaching _____

12. you (pl., for.) used to take _____

_____

13. we were not listening _____

_____

14. he used to sell _____

15. you (pl., for.) were opening _____

_____

16. were they receiving? _____

17. we were attending _____

18. you (s., fam.) used to study _____

_____

19. he was reading _____

20. they were living _____

21. you (pl., for.) were not hiding _____

_____

22. I used to receive _____

23. they did not understand _____

_____

24. I was eating _____

25. you (s., for.) used to sell _____

_____

26. you (s., fam.) were not taking _____

_____

27. they were listening _____

28. was he attending? _____

29. you (pl., fam.) used to need _____

_____

30. she was answering _____

_____

Preterit

The preterit is formed in regular verbs by adding the preterit endings to the stem.

	1	*2*	*3*
	hablar	**comer**	**partir**
yo	habl *é* I spoke, I did speak	com *í* I ate,	part *í* I left, did
tú	habl *aste* you spoke, etc.	com *iste* did eat	part *iste* leave
Ud.	habl *ó*	com *ió*	part *ió*
él(ella)	habl *ó*	com *ió*	part *ió*
nosotros	habl *amos*	com *imos*	part *imos*
vosotros	habl *asteis*	com *isteis*	part *isteis*
Uds.	habl *aron*	com *ieron*	part *ieron*
ellos	habl *aron*	com *ieron*	part *ieron*

Note: First- and third-person singular forms in all conjugations require a written accent. First-person plural forms of -*ar* and -*ir* verbs are identical to the present. As with the imperfect, endings for -*er* and -*ir* verbs are identical.

In this manual *I spoke* will be translated with the preterit as will *I did speak*. In negative or interrogative verbs, *I did not....* or *did I....* may indicate either imperfect or preterit.

Para practicar

Write the preterit of each verb that corresponds to the subject indicated:

yo

viajar	trabajar	estudiar	comer	vender	insistir
_____	_____	_____	_____	_____	_____

recibir

_____

tú

unir	acabar	comprar	romper	correr	abrir
_____	_____	_____	_____	_____	_____

tomar

_____

Ud.

comer	asistir	echar	preparar	subir	pasar
_____	_____	_____	_____	_____	_____

trabajar

_____

Pepe

viajar	hablar	aprender	resistir	llamar	responder
_____	_____	_____	_____	_____	_____

echar

_____

nosotros

trabajar	comprar	amar	vender	beber	correr
_____	_____	_____	_____	_____	_____

vivir

_____

tú y él

estudiar	comer	abrir	tomar	viajar	subir
_____	_____	_____	_____	_____	_____

pasar

_____

Uds.

trabajar	comprar	hablar	aprender	temer	escribir
_____	_____	_____	_____	_____	_____

viajar

_____

ellos

guardar	comprender	asistir	abrir	pasar	echar
_____	_____	_____	_____	_____	_____

beber

_____

Aplicación

A. Write the following infinitives in the preterit and in the person indicated by the subject.

1. yo (llevar) _____

2. nosotros (abrir) _____

3. tú (llegar) _____

4. Pepe y Juan (comer) _____

5. ella (beber) _____

6. tú y él (meter) _____

7. María y Elena (viajar) _____

8. Ud. (vivir) _____

9. mis amigos (pasar) _____

10. Uds. (vender) _____

11. yo (abrir) _____

12. Pablo (asistir) _____

13. ellos (recibir) _____

14. nosotras (tomar) _____

15. vosotros (temer) _____

16. ella (abrir) _____

17. Juan y él (escribir) _____

18. Uds. (necesitar) _____

B. Write (1) the preterit and (2) the imperfect of each verb given in the present.

1. tomamos _____

2. enseñan _____

3. Ud. contesta _____

4. reciben _____

5. aprende _____

6. asisto _____

7. tememos _____

8. venden _____

9. aprendo _____

10. contesto _____

11. Uds. toman _____

12. abre _____

13. necesita _____

14. recibes _____

15. trabaja _____

16. echan _____

17. suben _____

18. comprendo _____

16

A. Write the following infinitives in the preterit and in the person indicated by the subject. (*continued*)

19. tú (vender) _____

20. nosotros (beber) _____

21. ellos (aprender) _____

22. yo (tomar) _____

23. ella (estudiar) _____

24. Ud. (beber) _____

25. yo (recibir) _____

B. Write (1) the preterit and (2) the imperfect of each verb given in the present. (*continued*)

19. corre _____

20. trabajo _____

21. Ud. prepara _____

22. guardan _____

23. pasamos _____

24. viajo _____

25. echas _____

Mastery Test

Write in the preterit, using infinitives on page 6.

1. we answered _____

2. they sold _____

3. I learned _____

4. did you (s., fam.) listen? _____

_____

5. she did not ask _____

6. you (s., for.) hid _____

7. we took _____

8. they did not drink _____

9. we attended _____

10. I did teach _____

11. you (s., fam.) asked _____

12. they worked _____

13. you (pl., for.) joined _____

14. I lived _____

15. you (pl., fam.) answered _____

_____

16. you (pl., for.) did write _____

_____

17. she understood _____

18. they did not learn _____

19. we wrote _____

20. did he study? _____

21. you (s., fam.) sold _____

22. he taught _____

23. he attended _____

24. I sold _____

25. you (pl., fam.) did live _____

_____

26. they received _____

27. I attended _____

28. they asked _____

29. we drank _____

30. you (s., for.) studied _____

31. I did not answer _____

32. did you (pl., for.) open? _____

_____

33. they did not understand _____

_____

34. you (s., fam.) did not need _____

_____

35. we sold _____

36. did you (s., for.) take? _____

_____

37. we did not receive _____

38. she feared _____

39. I wrote _____

40. did you (pl., fam.) ask? _____

18

Repaso (Present, imperfect, preterit)

Write in Spanish, using the infinitives below and on page 6.

echar to throw
viajar to travel
pasar to pass, spend
guardar to keep

preparar to prepare
responder to reply, respond
correr to run
subir to go up

1. they used to live _____

2. I was opening _____

3. they did work _____

4. we were going up _____

5. I understand _____

6. they did not take _____

7. he was running _____

8. they answered _____

9. I work _____

10. you (s., fam.) prepared _____

_____

11. you (pl., for.) used to study _____

_____

12. they keep _____

13. we were spending _____

14. I traveled _____

15. you (s., for.) need _____

16. I was not living _____

17. you (pl., for.) used to open _____

_____

18. he used to write _____

19. I go up _____

20. he did understand _____

21. I was writing _____

22. you (s., fam.) respond _____

23. we understood _____

24. you (pl., fam.) did not learn _____

_____

25. they are preparing _____

26. we learn _____

27. we ran _____

28. you (pl., for.) were spending _____

_____

29. they did work _____

30. we attend _____

31. we were not writing _____

32. I threw _____

33. we were studying _____

34. I worked _____

35. we were living _____

36. we kept _____

37. you (s., fam.) understood _____

_____

38. they attended _____

39. we used to sell _____

40. I am spending _____

41. I lived _____

42. you (s., fam.) fear _____

43. she listened _____

44. you (pl., fam.) did not keep _____

_____

45. he is drinking _____

46. they used to keep _____

47. he left _____

48. you (s., for.) feared _____

49. we went up _____

50. I do not answer _____

Future

The future of regular verbs is formed by adding the future endings to the full infinitive or, in some irregular verbs, to a modified form of the infinitive.

	1 hablar	*2* comer	*3* partir
yo	hablar *é* I will speak	comer *é* I will eat	partir *é* I will leave
tú	hablar *ás*		partir *ás*
Ud.	hablar *á*	comer *ás*	partir *á*
él(ella)	hablar *á*	comer *á*	partir *á*
nosotros	hablar *emos*	comer *á*	partir *emos*
vosotros	hablar *éis*	comer *emos*	partir *éis*
Uds.	hablar *án*	comer *éis*	partir *án*
ellos	hablar *án*	comer *án*	partir *án*
		comer *án*	

Note: Future endings are the same for all three conjugations of verbs. All forms of the future except the first-person plural have a written accent.

Para practicar

Write the future form of each verb that corresponds to the subject indicated:

yo

comprar	hablar	leer	vivir	sentir	ser
_____	_____	_____	_____	_____	_____

asistir

_____

tú

estudiar	encontrar	correr	tomar	vender	conocer
_____	_____	_____	_____	_____	_____

partir

_____

Ud.

enseñar	perder	dormir	aprender	recibir	abrir
_____	_____	_____	_____	_____	_____

necesitar

_____

Juan

dudar	creer	amar	escribir	guardar	correr
_____	_____	_____	_____	_____	_____

subir

_____

nosotros

contestar	temer	preguntar	subir	viajar	aprender
_____	_____	_____	_____	_____	_____

vivir

_____

vosotros

preparar	echar	contestar	trabajar	viajar	responder
_____	_____	_____	_____	_____	_____

amar

_____

Uds.

comprar	leer	sentir	recibir	decidir	andar
_____	_____	_____	_____	_____	_____

pasar

_____

los niños

preparar   aprender   echar   viajar   contestar   correr

_____   _____   _____   _____   _____   _____

marchar

_____

Aplicación

A. Change the infinitive to correspond to the person indicated by the subject. Make all verbs future.

1. él (hablar) _____

2. nosotros (estar) _____

3. ella (ser) _____

4. Uds. (encontrar) _____

5. Juan (leer) _____

6. yo (dudar) _____

7. nosotros (perder) _____

8. tú (enseñar) _____

9. vosotros (dormir) _____

10. Ud. (andar) _____

11. tú (decidir) _____

12. yo (comprar) _____

13. él (vivir) _____

14. Ud. (sentir) _____

15. María (beber) _____

16. vosotros (estudiar) _____

17. él (abrir) _____

18. tú (vender) _____

19. ellos (escuchar) _____

20. Uds. (aprender) _____

21. ella (necesitar) _____

22. Ud. (contestar) _____

23. nosotras (temer) _____

24. yo (tomar) _____

25. tú (recibir) _____

B. Change all verbs to future and translate new form into English.

1. (ellos) vivían _____

2. abrí _____

_____   _____

3. subimos _____

_____

4. comprendías _____

_____

5. aprendimos _____

_____

6. (ellos) trabajaron _____

_____

7. Ud. corría _____

_____

8. (ellas) contestaban _____

_____

9. trabajé _____

_____

10. preparabais _____

_____

11. pasábamos _____

_____

12. viajo _____

_____

13. echabas _____

_____

14. partí _____

_____

15. abríais _____

_____

16. Uds. escribían _____

_____

17. subí _____

_____

18. (ella) comprendió _____

_____

19. corrimos _____

_____

20. Ud. contestó _____

_____

21. tomamos _____

_____

22. (ellos) enseñaron _____

_____

23. acababas _____

_____

24. (él) trabajaba _____

_____

25. escribí _____

_____

Mastery Test

Write in Spanish in the tense indicated by the English, using the infinitives below.

admirar   to admire   *llamar*   to call   *discutir*   to discuss   *ofender*   to offend
adornar   to adorn   *limpiar*   to clean   *insistir*   to insist   *emprender*   to undertake
molestar   to bother   *cubrir*   to cover   *decidir*   to decide

1. you (s., fam.) will adorn _____

_____

2. I was admiring _____

3. you (pl., fam.) will offend _____

_____

4. he bothers _____

5. you (pl., for.) will discuss _____

_____

6. I insisted _____

7. he will discuss _____

8. we will undertake _____

9. they will clean _____

10. you (pl., for.) are calling _____

_____

11. I will admire _____

12. he adorned _____

13. you (s., fam.) bother _____

_____

14. I will discuss _____

15. they insisted _____

16. they were covering _____

17. we will cover _____

18. we admired _____

19. you (pl., for.) undertook _____

_____

20. we insist _____

21. they discussed _____

22. we will clean _____

23. he was cleaning _____

24. I decided _____

25. she is calling _____

26. we were offending _____

27. we will call _____

28. you (s., for.) did discuss _____

_____

29. we will not admire _____

30. they do not call _____

31. you (pl., fam.) are deciding _____

_____

32. I covered _____

33. you (s., for.) will not discuss _____

_____

34. we will not decide _____

35. will you (s., fam.) clean? _____

_____

36. you (pl., fam.) will not insist _____

_____

37. they will cover _____

38. you (pl., for.) cleaned _____

_____

39. we were insisting _____

40. he offended _____

Conditional

The conditional is formed adding the conditional endings to the full infinitive or, in some irregular verbs, to a modified form of the infinitive.

	1 hablar		*2* comer		*3* partir	
yo	hablar *ía*	I should,	comer *ía*	I should,	partir *ía*	I should,
tú	hablar *ías*	would speak,	comer *ías*	would eat	partir *ías*	would
Ud.	hablar *ía*	etc.	comer *ía*		partir *ía*	leave
él(ella)	hablar *ía*		comer *ía*		partir *ía*	
nosotros	hablar *íamos*		comer *íamos*		partir *íamos*	
vosotros	hablar *íais*		comer *íais*		partir *íais*	
Uds.	hablar *ían*		comer *ían*		partir *ían*	
ellos	hablar *ían*		comer *ían*		partir *ían*	

Note: Conditional endings are identical to the *-er* and *-ir* imperfect endings, but are added to the full infinitive, not the stem. Conditional endings are the same for all conjugations.

All conditional forms must have a written accent.

Para practicar

Write the conditional form that corresponds to the subject indicated:

yo

admirar	decidir	trabajar	vivir	beber	abrir
_____	_____	_____	_____	_____	_____

morir

_____

tú

adornar	ofender	responder	estudiar	vender	escribir
_____	_____	_____	_____	_____	_____

sentir

_____

Ud.

molestar	emprender	correr	necesitar	aprender	llevar
_____	_____	_____	_____	_____	_____

partir

_____

él

llamar	echar	aprender	contestar	temer	sacar
_____	_____	_____	_____	_____	_____

hablar

_____

Luisa y yo

limpiar	viajar	comprender	preguntar	leer	tocar
_____	_____	_____	_____	_____	_____

comer

_____

tú y Juan

cubrir	pasar	subir	enseñar	creer	conocer
_____	_____	_____	_____	_____	_____

meter

_____

Uds.

discutir	guardar	abrir	escuchar	recibir	traer
_____	_____	_____	_____	_____	_____

pedir

_____

ellas

insistir	preparar	escribir	tomar	asistir	dormir
————————	————————	————————	————————	————————	————————

rogar

————————

Aplicación

A. Change the infinitives to the conditional, according to the person of the subject.

1. ellas (admirar) ————————————

2. Ud. (discutir) ————————————

3. tú (cubrir) ————————————

4. yo (limpiar) ————————————

5. tú y Juan (vender) ————————————

6. él (preguntar) ————————————

7. él y ella (vender) ————————————

8. nosotros (estudiar) ————————————

9. mi amigo y yo (vivir) ————————————

10. María (temer) ————————————

11. Pepe (abrir) ————————————

12. ellas (tomar) ————————————

13. nosotras (escribir) ————————————

14. María y él (contestar) ————————————

————————————————————————

15. Uds. (temer) ————————————

B. a) Change from the future to the conditional and translate.

1. contestaremos ————————————

2. aprenderé ————————————

3. (ellos) escucharán ————————————

4. (él) leerá ————————————

5. esconderemos ————————————

6. escribiréis ————————————

7. (Uds.) estudiarán ————————————

8. venderé ————————————

9. (ella) enseñará ————————————

10. (ellas) comprenderán ————————————

b) Change from the imperfect to the conditional and translate.

1. (Uds.) vivían ————————————

2. (él) abría ————————————

3. (ellos) trabajaban ————————————

4. subíamos ————————————

16. tú (llevar) _____

17. yo (beber) _____

18. Ud. (aprender) _____

19. él (echar) _____

20. ellos (viajar) _____

21. vosotros (necesitar) _____

22. Uds. (escuchar) _____

23. nosotras (enseñar) _____

24. ellas (asistir) _____

25. tú (recibir) _____

5. (él) comprendía _____

6. aprendíais _____

7. (él) corría _____

8. preparabas _____

9. guardábamos _____

10. (ella) viajaba _____

Mastery Test

Write in Spanish to correspond to the English tense and person.

1. you (s., fam.) will decide _____

_____

2. I should bother _____

3. you (s., for.) were adorning _____

_____

4. would he offend? _____

5. I insisted _____

6. we would discuss _____

7. they admired _____

8. he would not adorn _____

9. I will offend _____

10. they were offending _____

11. would she clean? _____

12. they undertake _____

13. they would admire _____

14. I will clean _____

15. you (pl., for.) would bother _____

_____

16. we will not cover _____

17. he covers _____

18. they would decide _____

19. will you (s., fam.) admire? _____

_____

20. we admired _____

21. they were insisting _____

22. I would not insist _____

23. you (pl., for.) cleaned _____

_____

24. she would decide _____

25. you (s., fam.) will insist _____

_____

26. would they call? _____

27. you (pl., fam.) would cover _____

_____

28. we will bother _____

29. they would not offend _____

_____

30. will I decide? _____

Progressive Tenses

Progressive tenses are compound tenses consisting of the appropriate tenses of *estar* and the present participle.

Present Participle: The present participle is formed by adding the ending *-ando* or *-iendo* to the infinitive stem.

1	2	3
hablar	**comer**	**partir**
habl *ando* speaking	com *iendo* eating	part *iendo* leaving

Note: The present participle has only one form; it does not distinguish person or number.

Estar to be (in a state or condition) (see page 104 for complete verb).

Present Progressive: The present progressive is formed with the present tense of *estar* plus the present participle. It is used to describe action thought of as in *progress*.

yo	*estoy*	*hablando*, com*iendo*, part*iendo*	I am (in the act of) speaking, eating,
tú	*estás*	habl*ando*, com*iendo*, part*iendo*	leaving
Ud.	*está*	habl*ando*, com*iendo*, part*iendo*	you are speaking, eating, leaving.
él(ella)	*está*	habl*ando*, com*iendo*, part*iendo*	
nosotros	*estamos*	habl*ando*, com*iendo*, part*iendo*	
vosotros	*estáis*	habl*ando*, com*iendo*, part*iendo*	
Uds.	*están*	habl*ando*, com*iendo*, part*iendo*	
ellos	*están*	habl*ando*, com*iendo*, part*iendo*	

Past Progressive: The past progressive is formed with the imperfect tense of *estar* pluš he present participle. It describes action which *was* in progress at a given moment in the past.

yo	*estaba*	habl*ando*, com*iendo*, part*iendo*	I was (in the act of) speaking, eating,
tú	*estabas*	habl*ando*, com*iendo*, part*iendo*	leaving
Ud.	*estaba*	habl*ando*, com*iendo*, part*iendo*	you were speaking, etc.
él(ella)	*estaba*	habl*ando*, com*iendo*, part*iendo*	
nosotros	*estábamos*	habl*ando*, com*iendo*, part*iendo*	
vosotros	*estabais*	habl*ando*, com*iendo*, part*iendo*	
Uds.	*estaban*	habl*ando*, com*iendo*, part*iendo*	
ellos	*estaban*	habl*ando*, com*iendo*, part*iendo*	

Note: The present and past progressive tenses are used to express present or past (imperfect) action when that action is thought of as *continuing* or *in progress*. They are thus a more vivid, dramatic substitute for the present and imperfect, respectively. The *estar* verb indicates the person and number of the subject; the participle *always* remains the same.

Para practicar

Write the present participles of the following infinitives:

admirar	adornar	subir	cubrir	acabar	correr
_____	_____	_____	_____	_____	_____

responder	tomar	sacar	decidir	dar
_____	_____	_____	_____	_____

Write the present progressive form that corresponds to the subject:

yo

abrir	llevar	perder	buscar	estudiar	beber
_____	_____	_____	_____	_____	_____

tú

vivir	aprender	tomar	escribir	trabajar	enseñar
_____	_____	_____	_____	_____	_____

Uds.

vender	abrir	contestar	asistir	escuchar	entrar
_____	_____	_____	_____	_____	_____

nosotros

recibir	echar	admirar	pasar	responder	correr
_____	_____	_____	_____	_____	_____

Aplicación

A. Write the past progressive form for the subject indicated.

1. Juan (llevar) _____

2. tú (estudiar) _____

3. vosotros (trabajar) _____

B. Change the present and imperfect verbs so that they express action in progress, keeping original subject.

1. reciben _____

2. trabajábamos _____

3. abrís _____

4. Pepe y yo (subir) _____

5. ellas (correr) _____

6. mi amigo (escuchar) _____

_____

7. los niños (jugar) _____

8. nosotros (escribir) _____

9. tú (comer) _____

10. ella (partir) _____

11. ella y yo (tomar) _____

12. él y ella (acabar) _____

13. yo (responder) _____

14. ellos (decidir) _____

15. él (cubrir) _____

4. preguntabais _____

5. no escuchaba _____

6. vivimos _____

7. bebe _____

8. Uds. asistían _____

9. vendes _____

10. Ud. no tomaba _____

11. enseñaba _____

12. contestáis _____

13. Ud. estudia _____

14. no comía _____

15. aprendo _____

Mastery Test

Express each English verb two ways:

1. I was admiring _____ _____

2. you (s., fam.) are deciding _____ _____

3. he was cleaning _____ _____

4. they were insisting _____ _____

5. they are not preparing _____ _____

6. you (s., for.) are calling _____ _____

7. they were covering _____ _____

8. were you (pl., for.) adorning? _____ _____

9. he is drinking   _____   _____

10. we were living   _____   _____

11. you (s., fam.) were not writing   _____   _____

12. I am spending   _____   _____

13. they are studying   _____   _____

14. we were spending   _____   _____

15. are you (pl., fam.) going up?   _____   _____

16. I was opening   _____   _____

17. was he running?   _____   _____

18. I was not living   _____   _____

19. we are not writing   _____   _____

Repaso (Future, conditional, progressive)

Write in Spanish:

1. you (pl., for.) will attend _____ _____

2. I was admiring _____

3. you (s., fam.) will offend _____ _____

4. I should bother _____

5. you (pl., fam.) are looking for _____ _____

6. you (s., for.) would not discuss _____ _____

7. I was insisting _____

8. she is studying _____

9. I will go up _____

10. he would admire _____

11. they were responding _____ _____

12. he is not bothering _____

13. will they discuss? _____

14. he was working _____

15. you (s., fam.) are not running _____

_____

16. he will listen _____

17. she was entering _____

18. we are spending _____

19. we would cover _____

20. they were cleaning _____

21. I will not open _____

22. you (pl., fam.) would lose _____

_____

23. you (s., for.) are calling _____

_____

24. he will clean _____

25. you (s., fam.) will teach _____

_____

26. you (pl., fam.) are working _____

_____

27. he will throw _____

28. I was writing _____

29. they are drinking _____

30. she would admire _____

31. we were calling _____

32. he was discussing _____

33. I will admire _____

34. you (s., for.) would bother _____

_____

35. they will spend _____

36. you (pl., for.) would write _____

_____

37. they were deciding _____

38. he will respond _____

Perfect Tenses

The perfect tenses are compound tenses, consisting in all cases of a form of the verb *haber* plus the past participle.

Past Participle: The past participle of regular verbs is formed by adding *-ado* or *-ido* to the stem.

1	*2*	*3*
hablar	**comer**	**partir**
habl *ado* spoken	com *ido* eaten	part *ido* left

The past participle does not change its ending to correspond to person and number in the perfect tenses.

Haber: *to have* is an irregular verb (see pages 104–5) which is used only in idiomatic expressions and as part of the perfect tenses.

Present Perfect: The present perfect is formed with the present tense of *haber* plus the past participle.

yo	*he* hablado I have spoken	*he* comido I have eaten	*he* partido I have left
tú	*has* hablado	*has* comido	*has* partido
Ud.	*ha* hablado	*ha* comido	*ha* partido
él(ella)	*ha* hablado	*ha* comido	*ha* partido
nosotros	*hemos* hablado	*hemos* comido	*hemos* partido
vosotros	*habéis* hablado	*habéis* comido	*habéis* partido
Uds.	*han* hablado	*han* comido	*han* partido
ellos	*han* hablado	*han* comido	*han* partido

Note: The same form of *haber* is used with all three conjugations. Negatives are formed by placing *no* before the *haber* verb.

Pluperfect: The pluperfect (past perfect) is formed with the imperfect of *haber* plus the past participle.

yo *había* hablado	I had spoken
había comido	I had eaten
había partido	I had left

The imperfect of *haber* is formed regularly (see page 8). What are the other forms of the pluperfect of *hablar*?

_____ _____ _____ _____ _____ _____

_____

Future Perfect: The future perfect is formed with the future of *haber* and the past participle.

yo *habré* hablado I will have spoken
habré comido   I will have eaten
habré partido   I will have left

The future of *haber* is formed by adding the future endings to the stem *habr-*. What are all the forms of the future perfect of *comer*?

_____ _____ _____ _____ _____ _____

_____ _____

What is the English translation of each of the preceding forms? _____

_____

_____

Conditional Perfect: The conditional perfect is formed with the conditional of *haber* and the past
participle.

yo *habría* hablado, comido, partido I would have spoken, eaten, left

The conditional of *haber* is formed by adding the conditional endings (see page 26) to the future stem *habr-*. What are all the forms of the conditional perfect of *partir*?

_____ _____ _____ _____ _____ _____

_____ _____

What are the English translations? _____

_____

Para practicar

Write the infinitives in (1) the present perfect, (2) pluperfect, (3) future perfect, and (4) conditional perfect, in the subject indicated:

1. yo (aprender)   _____ _____ _____ _____

2. ellos (limpiar) _____ _____ _____ _____

3. él (vivir)   _____ _____ _____ _____

4. nosotros (comprar) _____ _____ _____ _____

5. tú (asistir) _____ _____ _____ _____

6. ellos (vender) _____ _____ _____ _____

7. nosotros (tomar) _____ _____ _____ _____

8. él (aprender) _____ _____ _____ _____

9. Ud. (beber) _____ _____ _____ _____

10. ella (contestar) _____ _____ _____ _____

11. vosotros (recibir) _____ _____ _____ _____

12. ellos (preparar) _____ _____ _____ _____

13. nosotros (enseñar) _____ _____ _____ _____

14. tú (temer) _____ _____ _____ _____

15. Ud. (preguntar) _____ _____ _____ _____

16. Uds. (estudiar) _____ _____ _____ _____

17. él (pasar) _____ _____ _____ _____

18. nosotros (subir) _____ _____ _____ _____

19. Uds. (salir) _____ _____ _____ _____

20. tú (guardar) _____ _____ _____ _____

21. yo (esperar) _____ _____ _____ _____

22. vosotros (trabajar) _____ _____ _____ _____

23. ellos (vivir) _____ _____ _____ _____

24. Ud. (partir) _____ _____ _____ _____

25. ella (acabar) _____ _____ _____ _____

Aplicación

Change each simple tense verb to the corresponding perfect tense. Example: *como   he comido*; *hablé* or *hablaba   había hablado*; *tomaré   habré tomado*; *partirías   habrías partido*

1. Ud. comprende _____
2. vendías _____
3. escucharon _____
4. subirán _____
5. pregunta _____
6. Ud. discutirá _____
7. aprendían _____
8. Ud. estudió _____
9. escribes _____
10. guardaremos _____
11. admirarían _____
12. echaréis _____
13. temiste _____
14. asisto _____
15. tomábamos _____
16. prepararías _____
17. bebió _____
18. viviremos _____
19. corremos _____
20. viajará _____
21. decidirías _____
22. contestabais _____
23. partisteis _____
24. limpiaré _____
25. molestaríais _____

Mastery Test

Translate into Spanish:

1. I will have learned _____
2. he had cleaned _____
3. we have bought _____
4. they had lived _____
5. he would have run _____
6. I have asked _____
7. you (s., fam.) will have received _____
8. you (s., fam.) had feared _____
9. he has attended _____
10. they would have sold _____

11. we will have taken _____

12. you (s., for.) have answered _____

_____

13. I have needed _____

_____

14. you (pl., for.) would have asked _____

_____

15. they have spent _____

16. you (s., fam.) will have discussed _____

_____

17. they have received _____

18. he would have decided _____

_____

19. they will have listened _____

_____

20. we will have entered _____

21. you (s., for.) would have attended _____

_____

22. you (pl., fam.) had understood _____

_____

23. we have lived _____

24. you (pl., for.) will have worked _____

_____

25. he had taken _____

Repaso (Indicative tenses)

Translate into Spanish:

1. you (s., fam.) answer _____

_____

2. they used to live _____

3. I was opening _____

4. you (pl., fam.) are selling _____

_____

5. I will admire _____

6. they did work _____

7. he asks _____

8. you (pl., for.) will not offend _____

_____

9. we were going up _____

10. they do not sell _____

11. I should bother _____

12. I was understanding _____

13. we study _____

14. are you (pl., fam.) adorning? _____

_____

15. you (pl., for.) were learning _____

_____

16. we do not live _____

17. you (s., for.) discuss _____

18. he was running _____

19. does she need? _____

20. they bothered _____

21. they did not answer _____

22. she fears _____

23. we insisted _____

24. I did work _____

25. I will throw _____

26. you (pl., fam.) used to prepare _____

_____

27. he opens _____

28. you (s., for.) were admiring _____

_____

29. they kept _____

30. I will offend _____

31. we were spending _____

32. he would adorn _____

33. we will clean _____

34. we write _____

35. they were covering _____

36. you (pl., for.) were throwing _____

_____

37. they will fear _____

38. I was living _____

39. I used to travel _____

40. you (s., fam.) study _____

41. you (pl., for.) are calling _____

_____

42. you (pl., fam.) would open _____

_____

43. I drink _____

44. we were insisting _____

45. you (s., fam.) used to write _____

_____

46. will they call? _____

47. I went up _____

48. they would not discuss _____

_____

49. he did understand _____

50. they live _____

Present Subjunctive

Present: The present subjunctive of regular verbs is formed in the same way as the present indicative, except that *-ar* verbs use the endings of *-er* verbs, and *-er* and *-ir* verbs use *-ar* endings. All endings are added to the stem.

	1	*2*	*3*
	hablar	**comer**	**partir**
yo	habl *e* I may speak	com *a* I may eat	part *a* I may leave
tú	habl *es* you may speak	com *as* you may eat	part *as* you may leave
Ud.	habl *e* you may speak, etc.	com *a* you may eat	part *a*
él(ella)	habl *e*	com *a*	part *a*
nosotros	habl *emos*	com *amos*	part *amos*
vosotros	habl *éis*	com *áis*	part *áis*
Uds.	habl *en*	com *an*	part *an*
ellos	habl *en*	com *an*	part *an*

Note: The present subjunctive is also used for all negative commands, and affirmative commands with subjects *Ud.* and *Uds.* Thus: *coma* you (he, she) may eat, or eat (Ud.)! no partas is *you may not leave* or *do not leave*. In addition, the first-person plural may be translated *let us*......or *we may*......All of these variations will be found in the drill materials.

Para practicar

Write the present subjunctive form that corresponds to the subject indicated:

yo

echar	aprender	molestar	emprender	comprender	asistir
——————	——————	——————	——————	——————	——————

vivir

——————

tú

viajar	comprender	llamar	estudiar	beber	abrir
——————	——————	——————	——————	——————	——————

escribir

——————

Ud.

pasar	subir	limpiar	necesitar	vender	escribir
_____	_____	_____	_____	_____	_____

preparar

_____

ella

guardar	abrir	cubrir	contestar	aprender	llamar
_____	_____	_____	_____	_____	_____

tomar

_____

nosotros

preparar	escribir	discutir	preguntar	temer	trabajar
_____	_____	_____	_____	_____	_____

unir

_____

vosotros

trabajar	vivir	insistir	enseñar	leer	pasar
_____	_____	_____	_____	_____	_____

temer

_____

Uds.

responder	admirar	decidir	escuchar	vivir	guardar
_____	_____	_____	_____	_____	_____

viajar

_____

las chicas

correr	adornar	ofender	tomar	recibir	echar
_____	_____	_____	_____	_____	_____

subir

_____

Aplicación

Change from present indicative to present subjunctive.

1. lleva _____

2. vive _____

3. escriben _____

4. trabajáis _____

5. leen _____

6. hablo _____

7. Ud. estudia _____

8. llamamos _____

9. viajas _____

10. abre _____

11. creemos _____

12. manda _____

13. escribes _____

14. tomamos _____

15. comprenden _____

16. como _____

17. vives _____

18. asisto _____

19. Ud. nota _____

20. caminan _____

21. mete _____

22. observáis _____

23. partís _____

24. andas _____

25. insistimos _____

Mastery Test

Translate into Spanish:

1. I may not understand _____

_____

2. run! _____

3. he may ask _____

4. I may study _____

5. they may drink _____

6. he may sell _____

7. they may study _____

8. I may not sell _____

9. drink! _____

10. we may understand _____

11. I may receive _____

12. they may sell _____

13. you (pl., fam.) may study _____
_____

14. do (s., fam.) not ask! _____

15. we may not run _____

16. you (s., fam.) may receive _____
_____

17. I may teach _____

18. you (pl., fam.) may understand _____
_____

19. let us call _____

20. I may open _____

21. write! _____

22. she may travel _____

23. you (s., fam.) may take _____
_____

24. you (s., for.) may live _____
_____

25. let us insist _____

Imperfect Subjunctive

The imperfect subjunctive is formed by adding either the *-ra* or the *-se* endings, which are listed below, to the stem of the third-person plural preterit indicative.

	1 **hablar** *habla* ron	*2* **comer** *comie* ron	*3* **partir** *partie* ron
		-ra endings	
yo	habla *ra* I might speak	comie *ra* I might eat	partie *ra* I might leave
tú	habla *ras*	comie *ras*	partie *ras*
Ud.	habla *ra*	comie *ra*	partie *ra*
él(ella)	habla *ra*	comie *ra*	partie *ra*
nosotros	hablá *ramos*	comié *ramos*	partié *ramos*
vosotros	habla *rais*	comie *rais*	partie *rais*
Uds.	habla *ran*	comie *ran*	partie *ran*
ellos	habla *ran*	comie *ran*	partie *ran*
		-se endings	
yo	habla *se* I might speak	comie *se* I might eat	partie *se* I might leave
tú	habla *ses*	comie *ses*	partie *ses*
Ud.	habla *se*	comie *se*	partie *se*
él(ella)	habla *se*	comie *se*	partie *se*
nosotros	hablá *semos*	comié *semos*	partié *semos*
vosotros	habla *seis*	comie *seis*	partie *seis*
Uds.	habla *sen*	comie *sen*	partie *sen*
ellos	habla *sen*	comie *sen*	partie *sen*

Note: The first-person plural of both *-ra* and *-se* imperfect subjunctives must have a written accent. There is no difference in meaning between the two forms of the imperfect subjunctive and they may be used interchangeably, although the *-ra* form is the more common.

Para practicar

Write the *-ra* subjunctive form of the following infinitives according to the subject given.

yo

temer	asistir	abrir	acabar	escuchar	necesitar
_____	_____	_____	_____	_____	_____

Ud.

estudiar	abrir	aprender	tener	hablar	enseñar
_____	_____	_____	_____	_____	_____

nosotros

comprender	comer	entrar	partir	vivir	meter
_____	_____	_____	_____	_____	_____

Write these infinitives in the *-se* subjunctive that corresponds to the subject given.

tú

partir	preguntar	vivir	vender	hablar	guardar
_____	_____	_____	_____	_____	_____

ella

enseñar	tomar	comer	aprender	asistir	pasar
_____	_____	_____	_____	_____	_____

Uds.

hablar	contestar	estudiar	tomar	leer	escribir
_____	_____	_____	_____	_____	_____

Aplicación

A. Write the imperfect subjunctive of the infinitive in the person indicated.

1. él (hablar) _____

2. Elena y yo (vivir) _____

3. nosotros (correr) _____

4. tú (partir) _____

5. yo (pasar) _____

6. vosotros (esperar) _____

7. Uds. (acabar) _____

8. Ud. (caminar) _____

9. él (comprender) _____

10. Juan y Pedro (tomar) _____

B. Change from present to imperfect subjunctive.

1. contestemos _____

2. vendas _____

3. pregunte _____

4. aprenda _____

5. escuchen _____

6. Ud. escriba _____

7. aprendan _____

8. Ud. estudie _____

9. vivamos _____

10. tema _____

48

A. Write the imperfect subjunctive of the infinitive in the person indicated. (*continued*)

11. yo (escribir) _____

12. Ud. (amar) _____

13. tú (beber) _____

14. nosotros (comprar) _____

15. ellos (subir) _____

B. Change from present to imperfect subjunctive. (*continued*)

11. abra _____

12. enseñen _____

13. asista _____

14. tomemos _____

15. Uds. reciban _____

Mastery Test

Translate into Spanish:

1. I might teach _____

2. they might live _____

3. we might go up _____

4. I might not understand _____ _____

5. they might take _____

6. he might run _____

7. you (s., fam.) might answer _____ _____

8. I might work _____

9. you (pl., fam.) might not prepare _____ _____

10. you (s., for.) might study _____ _____

11. they might keep _____

12. we might not spend _____

13. I might travel _____

14. you (s., fam.) might need _____ _____

15. I might not live _____

16. you (pl. fam.) might open _____ _____

17. she might write _____

18. you (pl., for.) might respond _____ _____

19. he might fear _____

20. they might eat _____

Perfect Tenses of the Subjunctive

Present Perfect Subjunctive

The *present perfect subjunctive* is formed from the *present* subjunctive of *haber* plus the past participle. Present subjunctive of *haber* is found on page 104.

	1 **hablar**	*2* **comer**	*3* **partir**
yo	*haya* hablado	*haya* comido	*haya* partido
tú	*hayas* hablado	*hayas* comido	*hayas* partido
Ud.	*haya* hablado	*haya* comido	*haya* partido
él(ella)	*haya* hablado	*haya* comido	*haya* partido
nosotros	*hayamos* hablado	*hayamos* comido	*hayamos* partido
vosotros	*hayáis* hablado	*hayáis* comido	*hayáis* partido
Uds.	*hayan* hablado	*hayan* comido	*hayan* partido
ellos	*hayan* hablado	*hayan* comido	*hayan* partido
	(I, you, he, etc., may have spoken)	(I, you, he, etc., may have eaten)	(I, you, he, etc., may have left)

Note: As with other perfect tenses, the past participle does not change. The person and number of the verb form is indicated only by the *haber* verb.

Second person plural forms must have a written accent.

The negative is formed by placing *no* before the *haber* verb.

Pluperfect Subjunctive

The pluperfect subjunctive is formed from the imperfect (*-ra* or *-se*) subjunctive of *haber* plus the past participle. Imperfect subjunctive of *haber* is found on page 105.

	1	*2*	*3*
yo	*hubiera (hubiese)* hablado	*hubiera (hubiese)* comido	*hubiera (hubiese)* partido
tú	*hubieras* hablado	*hubieras* comido	*hubieras* partido
Ud.	*hubiera* hablado	*hubiera* comido	*hubiera* partido
él(ella)	*hubiera* hablado	*hubiera* comido	*hubiera* partido
nosotros	*hubiéramos* hablado	*hubiéramos* comido	*hubiéramos* partido
vosotros	*hubierais* hablado	*hubierais* comido	*hubierais* partido
Uds.	*hubieran* hablado	*hubieran* comido	*hubieran* partido
ellos	*hubieran* hablado	*hubieran* comido	*hubieran* partido
	(I, you, he, etc., might have spoken)	(I, you, he, etc., might have eaten)	(I, you, he, etc., might have left)

Para practicar

Write the *present perfect subjunctive* in the person indicated:

yo (estudiar) _____   tú (tomar) _____

María (necesitar) _____   ellos (vender) _____

Ud. (viajar) _____   tu amigo y tú (asistir) _____

nosotros (pasar) _____   Uds. (llamar) _____

Write in the *pluperfect subjunctive*:

yo (vivir) _____   nosotros (echar) _____

Uds. (guardar) _____   vosotros (asistir) _____

tú (caminar) _____   Ud. (aprender) _____

ellos (beber) _____

Aplicación

Change from simple to corresponding compound tense in the subjunctive. Example: *coma—haya comido*; *hablásemos—hubiéramos hablado*.

1. escuche _____

2. viviéramos _____

3. guardasen _____

4. trabajen _____

5. comprendamos _____

6. viviésemos _____

7. subieras _____

8. comprenda _____

9. no tomase _____

10. Ud. corra _____

11. respondieran _____

12. prepares _____

13. estudiarais _____

14. pasemos _____

15. viajéis _____

16. Uds. necesiten _____

17. suba _____

18. partiera _____

19. no aprendas _____

20. no conteste _____

21. temieras _____

22. asistiesen _____

23. no viva _____   25. llaméis _____

24. discutieses _____

Mastery Test

Translate into Spanish:

1. I may have learned _____

2. he might have taken _____

3. she might have cleaned _____

4. you (s., fam.) may have worked _____

5. we may have bought _____

6. we might have lived _____

7. they might have received _____

8. you (pl., fam.) might have understood _____

9. she might have attended _____

10. we may have taken _____

11. I may have needed _____

12. you (s., for.) might have asked _____

13. they may have lived _____

14. she might have run _____

15. we may have entered _____

16. I might have asked _____

17. they may have listened _____

18. you (pl., fam.) may have feared _____

19. she may have decided _____

20. you (pl., for.) might have answered _____

Repaso del subjuntivo

Write in Spanish:

1. I may understand

_____

2. you (pl., fam.) may have drunk

_____

3. we might have understood

_____

4. I may not receive

_____

5. I might teach

_____

6. we might run

_____

7. you (s., for.) might have received

_____

8. you (s., fam.) may understand

_____

9. we might not understand

_____

10. I may have studied

_____

11. I might not run

_____

12. we may have taught

_____

13. they may have sold

_____

14. they might have drunk

_____

15. I may not have received

_____

16. she might have received

_____

17. let us understand

_____

18. he may have drunk

_____

19. study! (s., for.)

_____

20. we might have received

_____

21. I may sell

_____

22. they might understand

_____

23. we may have studied

_____

24. you (pl., fam.) may not study

_____

25. I might study

_____

26. I may have asked

_____

27. you (s., fam.) may have sold

_____

28. you (pl., fam.) might have drunk

_____

29. I might not have taught

_____

30. we may study

_____

31. do not sell! (pl., fam.)

_____

32. I might understand

_____

33. she may have studied

_____

34. he might have drunk

_____

35. they might have taught

_____

36. let's not ask

_____

37. they might drink

_____

38. run! (pl.)

_____

39. they might run

_____

40. you (pl., for.) may have studied

_____

Reflexive Verbs

Reflexive verbs are verbs in which the object *reflects* the subject, that is, the subject does the action to itself. Therefore, in Spanish reflexive verbs, the object pronoun must change each time the person of the subject changes. The reflexive verb has the same forms as a nonreflexive verb, but the object pronoun is always included, in the same person as the ending of the verb indicates.

Present of Reflexive Verbs: levantar(se)   to get (oneself) up, to arise

yo	*me* levanto	I get (myself) up
tú	*te* levantas	you get (yourself) up
Ud.	*se* levanta	
él(ella)	*se* levanta	

nosotros *nos* levantamos

vostros *os* levantáis

Uds. *se* levantan

ellos *se* levantan

Reflexive pronouns are the same for verbs of all three conjugations. The infinitive indicates that the verb is reflexive by having *-se* attached to it (*levantarse*). The *se* is removed with the infinitive ending when the personal endings are attached. The reflexive is also the same form for all tenses of the verb.

Imperfect: yo me levantaba   I was getting up. Write the other forms of the imperfect, taking care to use the correct reflexive pronoun with each form (Imperfect, p. 8):

_____   _____   _____   _____

_____   _____   _____   _____

Preterit: yo me levanté   I got up. Write the other forms of the preterit (p. 13):

_____   _____   _____   _____

_____   _____   _____   _____

Future: yo me levantaré   I shall get up. Write the other forms of the future (p. 20):

_____   _____   _____   _____

_____   _____   _____   _____

Conditional: yo me levantaría   I would get up. Write the other forms of the conditional (p. 26):

_____   _____   _____   _____

_____   _____   _____   _____

Progressive Tenses: *yo me estoy levantando* or *yo estoy levantándome*   I am getting up.
  Note that the pronoun may either precede or follow in the progressive. Write the *yo* form of the *past* progressive in Spanish and translate into English:

yo _____   _____

Perfect Tenses: *Present*: *yo me he levantado*   I have gotten up. The pronoun precedes the *haber* verb in all perfect tenses. Change the present perfect to (1) pluperfect, (2) future perfect, and (3) conditional perfect, and translate each into English:

yo me he levantado: Translate:

(1) yo _____   (1) _____

(2) _____   (2) _____

(3) _____   (3) _____

Subjunctive: Present: *yo me levante*   I may get up. Write the other forms of present subjunctive:

_____   _____   _____   _____

_____   _____

Imperfect: *yo me levantara* (*me levantase*)   I might get up. Write the other forms of the imperfect subjunctive, first the *-ra* and then the *-se* forms:

tú _____   tú (-se) _____

Ud. _____   Ud. _____

él _____   él _____

_____   _____

_____   _____

_____   _____

_____   _____

Present Perfect: yo me haya levantado I may have gotten up. Write the singular forms of the present perfect subjunctive and translate into English:

yo _____ Trans. _____

tú _____ _____

Ud. _____ _____

él _____ _____

Pluperfect: yo me hubiera levantado I might have gotten up. Write the plural forms of the imperfect subjunctive (*-se* form) and translate into English:

nosotros _____ Trans. _____

vosotros _____ _____

Uds. _____ _____

ellos _____ _____

Aplicación

Two other verbs which are treated in a manner similar to *levantarse* are *lavarse* to wash, get washed, and *peinarse* to comb oneself, get combed.

A. Change the verbs so that they express the idea of a subject acting on itself:

1. lavéis _____

2. peinaban _____

3. levantó _____

4. peinemos _____

5. levantábamos _____

6. lavan _____

7. levantamos _____

8. hayan peinado _____

B. Change each simple tense to a corresponding compound tense, keeping the person of the original verb.

1. se levanten _____

2. nos levantamos _____

3. te peinas _____

4. os levantáis _____

5. nos peinaremos _____

6. me peiné _____

7. se levantaba _____

8. nos levantaríamos _____

9. lavabas _____

10. peiné _____

11. lavantáis _____

12. hubieras levantado _____

13. peina _____

14. lavaré _____

15. peinarías _____

9. se peinaron _____

10. se lave _____

11. os peinéis _____

12. nos lavemos _____

13. me levante _____

14. se levantarán _____

15. me lavaré _____

Mastery Test

Write in Spanish, using reflexive verbs:

1. he may have washed _____

2. they were washing _____

3. they comb their hair _____

4. he might wash _____

5. I had gotten up _____

6. they got up _____

7. they will have washed _____

8. I am combing my hair _____

9. they would have gotten up _____

10. I used to get up _____

11. I wash _____

12. he may get up _____

13. we shall wash _____

14. he has washed _____

15. we might comb our hair _____

16. they washed _____

17. I would wash _____

18. they get up _____

19. you (s., fam.) washed _____

20. they might have washed _____

Repaso de verbos regulares

A. Change each verb to represent more than one person in the same tense.

1. acabo _____

2. comprendiste _____

3. él temía _____

4. necesitaré _____

5. partirías _____

6. estoy enseñando _____

7. partes _____

8. Ud. hable _____

9. ha enseñado _____

10. hayas hablado _____

11. estaba lavándose _____

12. habías vendido _____

13. él hubiese asistido _____

14. bebieras _____

15. habrá preguntado _____

16. habrías tomado _____

17. escucha _____

18. he estudiado _____

19. habrás temido _____

20. aprenderá _____

21. comprendas _____

22. está viviendo _____

23. Ud. había acabado _____

24. contesté _____

25. Ud. vendiese _____

26. yo habría partido _____

27. abrías _____

28. Ud. entraría _____

29. estabas comiendo _____

30. Ud. haya tomado _____

B. Translate into English:

1. parto _____

2. Uds. escribieron _____

3. asistiréis _____

4. ellos vivían _____

5. tomaríamos _____

6. enseñasteis _____

7. él está estudiando _____

8. temeremos _____

9. Ud. estaba abriendo _____

_____

10. ella vendería _____

11. has asistido _____

12. Ud. ha comido _____

13. ellos habían comprendido _____

_____

14. estás escuchando _____

15. habremos tenido _____

16. yo había estudiado _____

17. estaba levantándome _____

_____

18. habrás hablado _____

19. bebiéramos _____

20. Ud. habría contestado _____

_____

21. comas _____

22. él escriba _____

23. él se haya lavado _____

24. aprendiésemos _____

25. hubieras estudiado _____

26. hayáis hablado _____

27. Uds. hubieran comido _____

_____

28. ellos temen _____

29. Uds. habrían llevado _____

_____

30. Uds. llevaban _____

C. Write in Spanish:

1. they fear _____

2. she might have left _____

3. you (s., fam.) used to eat _____

4. we may have spoken _____

5. did you (pl., fam.) speak? _____

6. I used to leave _____

7. we will learn _____

8. you (s., fam.) might take _____

9. he would not write _____

10. they understood _____

11. you (s., fam.) are answering _____

12. they would have left _____

13. you (pl., fam.) were speaking _____

14. I have studied _____

15. do not finish! (pl., fam.) _____

16. they had left _____

17. I will have taught _____

18. you (s., for.) will have lived _____

19. we are living _____

20. you (pl., for.) would have taught _____

21. let us fear _____

22. you (s., fam.) do not read _____

23. he might sell _____

24. you (pl., fam.) may not have eaten _____

25. he was selling _____

26. you (pl., fam.) might not have listened _____

27. I sell _____

28. will you (s., fam.) read? _____

29. they used to carry _____

30. you (s., fam.) wrote _____

31. you (pl., fam.) will attend _____

32. we would take _____

33. she is not studying _____

34. you (pl., fam.) were opening _____

35. you (s., for.) have not attended _____

36. I had understood _____

37. you (s., fam.) would carry _____

38. they will have studied _____

39. you (pl., for.) would not have needed _____

40. drink! (pl., for.) _____

41. we might not attend _____

42. you (s., fam.) have lived _____

43. he may have finished _____

44. you (pl., for.) might have learned _____

45. do you (pl., fam.) open? _____

46. I used to fear _____

47. you (s., fam.) had taken _____

48. they asked _____

49. you (s., for.) will enter _____

50. would you (s., fam.) read? _____

Stem-Changing Verbs—Class I

Stem-changing verbs change the last vowel of the stem under certain conditions.

In stem-changing verbs of Class I (-*ar* or -*er* verbs), the *e* or *o* of the stem changes to *ie* or *ue*, respectively, in all the forms of both the present indicative and the present subjunctive, except the *nosotros* and *vosotros* forms.

Present Indicative:

	1		*2*	
	pensar to think		**entender** to understand	
yo	*piens* o	I think, am thinking	*entiend* o	I understand, etc.
tú	*piens* as		*entiend* es	
Ud.	*piens* a		*entiend* e	
él(ella)	*piens* a		*entiend* e	
nosotros	pens amos		entend emos	
vosotros	pens áis		entend éis	
Uds.	*piens* an		*entiend* en	
ellos	*piens* an		*entiend* en	

Note: The stem is formed in the regular way when it is not accented. No other indicative tense except the present has an accented stem for regular verbs. The present is thus the only indicative tense in which this change occurs.

Present Subjunctive:

	1		*2*	
	contar to tell		**volver** to return	
yo	*cuent* e	I may tell	*vuelv* a	I may return
tú	*cuent* es		*vuelv* as	
Ud.	*cuent* e		*vuelv* a	
él(ella)	*cuent* e		*vuelv* a	
nosotros	cont emos		volv amos	
vosotros	cont éis		volv áis	
Uds.	*cuent* en		*vuelv* an	
ellos	*cuent* en		*vuelv* an	

What would the present subjunctive of (1) *pensar* (2) *entender* be?

(1) _____ _____ _____ _____ _____ _____

_____ _____

(2) _____ _____ _____ _____ _____ _____

_____ _____

What would the present indicative of (1) *contar* and (2) *volver* be?

(1) _____ _____ _____ _____ _____ _____

_____ _____

(2) _____ _____ _____ _____ _____ _____

_____ _____

Other Verbs of Class I:

calentar to warm
cerrar to close
mostrar to show
morder to bite
perder to lose
mover to move
revolver to stir, turnover

devolver to give back, return
encender to light
acertar to succeed, guess right
acordar to agree
acostar(se) to put (go) to bed
aprobar to approve
sentar(se) to seat (sit)

confesar to confess
costar to cost
*nevar** to snow
*llover** to rain
encontrar to find, meet

* This verb is used only in the third-person singular.

Para practicar

A. Write the infinitive in the *present indicative* in the subject indicated:

yo

cerrar	encontrar	mostrar	perder	revolver	encender
_____	_____	_____	_____	_____	_____

Uds.

confesar	acostarse	mover	devolver	acertar	acordar
_____	_____	_____	_____	_____	_____

nosotros

sentarse	contar	mostrar	perder	devolver	entender
_____	_____	_____	_____	_____	_____

B. Write the infinitives in the *present subjunctive* in the subject indicated:

tú

contar	pensar	morder	aprobar	devolver	entender
_____	_____	_____	_____	_____	_____

ellas

cerrar	encontrar	mostrar	perder	mover	encender
_____	_____	_____	_____	_____	_____

vosotros

entender	revolver	mostrar	mover	confesar	acordar
_____	_____	_____	_____	_____	_____

Mastery Test

A. Translate into English:

1. se acuestan _____

2. acuerdo _____

3. ella vuelve _____

4. Ud. caliente _____

5. mostremos _____

6. perdéis _____

7. Uds. revuelvan _____

8. enciendas _____

9. él aprobó _____

10. me sentaba _____

11. costó _____

12. nevará _____

13. confieso _____

14. ellos devuelven _____

15. cierre Ud. _____

B. Translate into Spanish:

1. you (pl., fam.) lost _____

2. they may understand _____

_____

3. we may meet _____

4. do you (s., fam.) close? _____

_____

5. you (s., fam.) do not understand _____

_____

6. they moved _____

7. I was moving _____

8. they may show _____

9. you (s., fam.) move _____

10. we warmed _____

11. I am lighting _____

12. they do not lose _____

13. I may bite _____

14. you (s., fam.) may stir _____

_____

15. it costs _____

Stem-Changing Verbs—Class II

In stem-changing verbs of Class II (-*ir* verbs), the *e* or *o* of the stem changes to *ie* or *ue* respectively, in all the forms of the present indicative tense, except the *nosotros* and *vosotros* forms, and to *i* or *u* in the third-person singular and plural of the preterit. In the present subjunctive, the *ie* and *ue* change to *i* and *u*, respectively, in the *nosotros* and *vosotros* forms.

Present:	**sentir** to feel	**dormir** to sleep
yo	*sient* o I feel, am feeling	*duerm* o I sleep, am sleeping
tú	*sient* es	*duerm* es
Ud.	*sient* e	*duerm* e
él(ella)	*sient* e	*duerm* e
nosotros	sent imos	dorm imos
vosotros	sent ís	dorm ís
Uds.	*sient* en	*duerm* en
ellos	*sient* en	*duerm* en

Present Participle: *sint* iendo   feeling   *durm* iendo   sleeping

Preterit:

yo	sent í I felt, did feel	dorm í I slept, did sleep
tú	sent iste	dorm iste
Ud.	*sint* ió	*durm* ió
él(ella)	*sint* ió	*durm* ió
nosotros	sent imos	dorm imos
vosotros	sent isteis	dorm isteis
Uds.	*sint* ieron	*durm* ieron
ellos	*sint* ieron	*durm* ieron

No other tenses of the indicative are affected.

Present Subjunctive:

yo	*sient* a I may feel	*duerm* a I may sleep
tú	*sient* as	*duerm* as
Ud.	*sient* a	*duerm* a
él(ella)	*sient* a	*duerm* a
nosotros	*sint* amos	*durm* amos
vosotros	*sint* áis	*durm* áis
Uds.	*sient* an	*duerm* an
ellos	*sient* an	*duerm* an

Imperfect Subjunctive: Since the imperfect subjunctive is formed from the stem of the third-person plural preterit, all forms reflect the same stem-change.

yo	*sint* iera	*sint* iese	I might	*durm* iera	*durm* iese	I might
tú	*sint* ieras	*sint* ieses	feel	*durm* ieras	*durm* ieses	sleep
Ud.	*sint* iera	*sint* iese		*durm* iera	*durm* iese	
él(ella)	*sint* iera	*sint* iese		*durm* iera	*durm* iese	
nosotros	*sint* iéramos	*sint* iésemos		*durm* iéramos	*durm* iésemos	
vosotros	*sint* ierais	*sint* ieseis		*durm* ierais	*durm* ieseis	
Uds.	*sint* ieran	*sint* iesen		*durm* ieran	*durm* iesen	
ellos	*sint* ieran	*sint* iesen		*durm* ieran	*durm* iesen	

Others:

advertir to notice   *mentir* to lie
consentir to consent   *morir* to die
divertir(se) to amuse (oneself), have fun   *herir* to wound

Para practicar

Change the infinitives to the tense and person indicated:

Present indicative **tú**

advertir	mentir	morir	herir	consentir
_____	_____	_____	_____	_____

Present Subjunctive **Ud.**

divertirse	sentir	dormir	mentir	morir
_____	_____	_____	_____	_____

Preterit **ellos**

herir	advertir	divertirse	dormir	consentir
_____	_____	_____	_____	_____

Imperfect Subjunctive **nosotros**

morir	sentir	mentir	dormir	advertir
_____	_____	_____	_____	_____

Present Participle

morir	herir	consentir	advertir	divertirse
_____	_____	_____	_____	_____

Mastery Test

A. Translate into English:

1. Ud. mentía _____

2. dormimos _____

3. ella murió _____

4. ellos mintieran _____

5. él había sentido _____

6. ellos se divierten _____

7. él hirió _____

8. él consienta _____

9. no advierto _____

10. Uds. mintieron _____

11. sentí _____

12. mueras _____

13. sintáis _____

14. ellos duerman _____

15. nos divirtamos _____

B. Translate into Spanish:

1. they do not wound _____

2. you (s., fam.) have slept _____

_____

3. we may consent _____

4. I might die _____

5. he may sleep _____

6. you (s., fam.) amused yourself _____

_____

7. we will lie _____

8. they were dying _____

9. he was feeling _____

10. he might sleep _____

11. I would consent _____

12. you (s., for.) noticed _____

13. I sleep _____

14. they might feel _____

15. you (pl., fam.) may amuse yourself _____

_____

Stem-Changing Verbs—Class III

In stem-changing verbs of Class III (-*ir* verbs), the *e* of the stem changes to *i* in all the forms of the present indicative tense, except the *nosotros* and *vosotros* forms, and in the third-person singular and plural of the preterit.

Pedir   to ask for

Present Indicative: *pido*, *pides*, *pide*, pedimos, pedís, *piden*   I ask for, etc.

Imperfect: pedía, etc.   I was looking for, etc.

Preterit: pedí, pediste, *pidió*, pedimos, pedisteis, *pidieron*   I asked for, etc.

Future: pediré, etc.   I will ask for, etc.

Conditional: pediría, etc.   I would ask for, etc.

Present Participle: *pidiendo*   asking for

Past Participle: pedido

Present Subjunctive: *pida*, *pidas*, *pida*, *pidamos*, *pidáis*, *pidan*   I may ask for, etc.

Imperfect Subjunctive: *pidiera* (*pidiese*), etc.   I might ask for, etc.

Present Perfect Subjunctive: haya pedido, etc.   I may have looked for, etc.

Pluperfect Subjunctive: hubiera (hubiese) pedido, etc.   I might have looked for, etc.

All Spanish forms not in italics are regular.

Others:	*gemir* to groan
impedir to prevent	*medir* to measure
repetir to repeat	*competir* to compete
servir to serve	
vestirse to get dressed, dress	

Para practicar

Change the infinitives to the tense and person indicated:

Present indicative   **Ud.**

impedir	competir	servir	medir
_____	_____	_____	_____

Present subjunctive   **vosotros**

gemir	pedir	impedir	competir
_____	_____	_____	_____

Preterit **ellos**

vestirse	servir	medir	impedir
_____	_____	_____	_____

Mastery Test

Translate into English:

1. ellos gimieran _____

2. me vista _____

3. él pediría _____

4. medíamos _____

5. midáis _____

6. impedimos _____

7. Ud. gimió _____

8. competiré _____

9. sirviéramos _____

10. él gime _____

11. mediste _____

12. sirvieron _____

13. compito _____

14. se visten _____

15. impidas _____

Repaso (Stem-changing verbs)

A. Write the *third-person singular present indicative* of the following infinitives:

ella

gemir	competir	cerrar	sentir	impedir	mostrar
_____	_____	_____	_____	_____	_____

encontrar	divertirse	sentarse	revolver
_____	_____	_____	_____

B. Write the *first-person plural present subjunctive* of the following infinitives:

nosotros

aprobar	medir	dormir	confesar	mentir	advertir
_____	_____	_____	_____	_____	_____

pedir	vestirse	repetir	consentir
_____	_____	_____	_____

C.   Write in Spanish:

1. they understand _____

2. we may consent _____

3. I may dress _____

4. he is not amusing himself _____

_____

5. we may close _____

6. you (s., fam.) asked for _____

_____

7. she did not notice _____

8. he meets _____

9. you (s., for.) might groan _____

_____

10. I may die _____

11. you (s., fam.) may move _____

_____

12. we might serve _____

13. they notice _____

14. I close _____

15. he competes _____

16. you (s., fam.) may show _____

_____

17. I might amuse myself _____

_____

18. they served _____

19. you (pl., fam.) do not lose _____

_____

20. she may sleep _____

21. he prevents _____

22. I may give back _____

23. they felt _____

24. you (pl., for.) may prevent _____

_____

25. does he understand? _____

26. they are not dying _____

27. she did not compete _____

28. it may snow _____

29. you (s., fam.) are lying _____

_____

30. they might ask for _____

Orthographic Changes

Orthographic-changing verbs change the spelling of certain consonants when it is necessary to maintain a uniform pronunciation of their stems.

Verbs ending in -car change c to qu before the letter e.

Buscar to look for

Present Indicative: busco, etc. I look for, etc. (p. 1)

Imperfect: buscaba, etc. I was looking for, etc. (p. 8)

Preterit: *busqué*, buscaste, buscó, etc. I looked for, etc. (p. 13)

Future: buscaré, etc. I will look for, etc. (p. 20)

Conditional: buscaría, etc. I would look for, etc. (p. 26)

Present Participle: buscando   looking for

Past Participle: buscado   looked for

Present Subjunctive: *busque, busques, busque, busquemos, busquéis, busquen*   I may look for, etc.

Imperfect Subjunctive: buscara (buscase), etc. I might look for, etc. (p. 46)

Present Perfect Subjunctive: haya buscado, etc. I may have looked for, etc. (p. 49)

Pluperfect Subjunctive: hubiera (hubiese) buscado, etc. I might have looked for, etc. (p. 49)

Verb forms not in italics are not affected.

Others:	*sacar* to take out
colocar to place	*secar* to dry
explicar to explain	*convocar* to call together
indicar to indicate	*replicar* to reply
marcar to mark	*pecar* to sin
mascar (*masticar*) to chew	
rascar to scratch	

Verbs ending in -*gar* change *g* to *gu* before the letter *e*. The *u* is not pronounced.

Pagar to pay

Present Indicative: pago, pagas, etc. I pay, etc.

Imperfect: pagaba, etc. I was paying, etc.

Preterit: *pagué*, pagaste, pagó, etc. I paid, etc.

Future: pagaré, etc. I will pay, etc.

Conditional: pagaría, etc. I would pay, etc.

Present Participle: pagando   paying

Past Participle: pagado   paid

Present Subjunctive: *pague, pagues, pague, paguemos, paguéis, paguen*   I may pay, etc.

Imperfect Subjunctive: pagara (pagase) I might pay, etc.

Present Perfect Subjunctive: haya pagado, etc.   I may have paid, etc.

Pluperfect Subjunctive: hubiera (hubiese) pagado, etc.   I might have paid, etc.

Others:

apagar to turn off, extinguish	*llegar* to arrive
arriesgar to risk	*obligar* to oblige
cargar to load	*vagar* to wander
castigar to punish	*colgar** to hang up
ahogar to drown	*rogar** to beg, ask
entregar to hand over	*negar** to deny
fatigar to tire	*cegar** to blind

* see page 85

Verbs ending in *-zar* change *z* to *c* before the letter *e*.

Rezar   to pray

Present Indicative: rezo, rezas, etc.   I pray, etc.

Imperfect: rezaba, etc.   I was praying, etc.

Preterit: *recé*, rezaste, rezó, etc.   I prayed, etc.

Future: rezaré, etc.   I will pray, etc.

Conditional: rezaría, etc.   I would pray, etc.

Present Participle: rezando   praying

Past Participle: rezado   prayed

Present Subjunctive: *rece, reces, rece, recemos, recéis, recen*,   I may pray, etc.

Imperfect Subjunctive: rezara (rezase), etc.   I might pray, etc.

Present Perfect Subjunctive: haya rezado, etc.   I may have prayed, etc.

Pluperfect Subjunctive: hubiera (hubiese) rezado, etc.   I might have prayed, etc.

Others:

abrazar to embrace	*rechazar* to reject
alcanzar to reach, achieve	*sollozar* to sob
amenazar to threaten	*empezar** to begin
analizar to analyze	*almorzar** to eat lunch
cruzar to cross	*tropezar** to stumble
lanzar to throw	

* see page 85

Verbs ending in *-guar* change *gu* to *gü* before *e*. The *u* requires a diaeresis (‥)before *e* to preserve the *u* sound.

Averiguar   to find out, verify

Present Indicative: averiguo, etc.   I find out, etc.

Imperfect: averiguaba, etc.   I was finding out, etc.

Preterit: *averigüé*, averiguaste, averiguó, etc.   I found out, etc.

Future: averiguaré, etc.   I will find out, etc.

Conditional: averiguaría, etc.   I would find out, etc.

Present Participle: averiguando   finding out

Past Participle: averiguado   found out

Present Subjunctive: *averigüe, averigües, averigüe, averigüemos, averigüéis, averigüen*   I may find out, etc.

Imperfect Subjunctive: averiguara (averiguase), etc.   I might find out, etc.

Present Perfect Subjunctive: haya averiguado, etc.   I may have found out, etc.

Pluperfect Subjunctive: hubiera (hubiese) averiguado, etc.   I might have found out, etc.

Others:

apaciguar   to pacify

menguar   to decrease

santiguar   to bless

Para practicar

Write in the *present subjunctive* in the person indicated:

tú:

secar	colocar	obligar	entregar	amenazar	analizar
_____	_____	_____	_____	_____	_____

averiguar	menguar
_____	_____

ellos

alcanzar	abrazar	llegar	castigar	arriesgar	rascar
_____	_____	_____	_____	_____	_____

replicar	explicar
_____	_____

Write in the *first-person singular preterit indicative*:

yo

explicar	sacar	indicar	negar	llegar	castigar
_____	_____	_____	_____	_____	_____

rogar	replicar	empezar	cruzar	rechazar	almorzar
_____	_____	_____	_____	_____	_____

marcar	apaciguar	santiguar
_____	_____	_____

Mastery Test

A. Translate into English:

1. él explique _____

2. Ud. marcara _____

3. yo apague _____

4. abracé _____

5. entregué _____

6. tropecemos _____

7. ellos sequen _____

8. castigues _____

9. Ud. rechace _____

10. averigües _____

11. tú repliques _____

12. carguemos _____

13. amenaces _____

14. mengüé _____

15. saqué _____

B. Translate into Spanish:

1. we may pacify _____

2. I paid _____

3. they may take out _____

4. I did not find out _____

5. you (s., fam.) may punish _____
_____

6. he may not place _____

7. I risked _____

8. we may tire _____

9. she may not reply _____

10. you (s., fam.) may cross _____
_____

11. you (pl., fam.) may beg _____
_____

12. I indicated _____

A.   Translate into English: (*continued*)

16. santigüemos _____

17. él llegue _____

18. Uds. analicen _____

19. apacigüen _____

20. él alcance _____

B.   Translate into Spanish: (*continued*)

13. he prays _____

14. you (s., fam.) may throw _____

_____

15. they may arrive _____

16. I did not explain _____

17. we may not analyze _____

18. you (pl., fam.) may reply _____

_____

19. I threw _____

20. I sobbed _____

Some verbs ending in -*cer* and -*cir* preceded by a consonant change *c* to *z* before *o* or *a*.

Vencer   to conquer

Present Indicative: *venzo*, vences, etc.   I conquer, etc.
Imperfect: vencía, etc.   I was conquering, etc.
Preterit: vencí, etc.   I conquered, etc.
Future: venceré, etc.   I will conquer, etc.
Conditional: vencería, etc.   I would conquer, etc.
Present Participle: venciendo   conquering
Past Participle: vencido   conquered
Present Subjunctive: *venza, venzas, venza, venzamos, venzáis, venzan*   I may conquer, etc.
Imperfect Subjunctive: venciera, (venciese), etc.   I might conquer, etc.
Present Perfect Subjunctive: haya vencido, etc.   I may have conquered, etc.
Pluperfect Subjunctive: hubiera (hubiese) vencido, etc.   I might have conquered, etc.

Others:

convencer   to convince
ejercer   to exercise
esparcir   to scatter

Verbs ending in *-ger* or *-gir* change *g* to *j* before an *o* or *a*.

Escoger   to choose

Present Indicative: *escojo*, escoges, etc.   I choose, etc.

Imperfect: escogía, etc.   I was choosing, etc.

Preterit: escogí, etc.   I chose, etc.

Future: escogeré, etc.   I will choose, etc.

Conditional: escogería, etc.   I would choose, etc.

Present Participle: escogiendo   choosing

Past Participle: escogido   chosen

Present Subjunctive: *escoja, escojas, escoja, escojamos, escojáis, escojan*   I may choose, etc.

Imperfect Subjunctive: escogiera (escogiese), etc.   I might choose, etc.

Present Perfect Subjunctive: haya escogido, etc.   I may have chosen, etc.

Pluperfect Subjunctive: hubiera (hubiese) escogido, etc.   I might have chosen, etc.

Others:

dirigir to direct	*acoger* to welcome
coger to catch, seize, take	*encoger* to shrink
fingir to pretend	*corregir* to correct*
exigir to demand	*elegir* to elect, choose*
infligir to inflict	* see page 86

Verbs ending in *-guir* drop the *u* before *o* or *a*.

Distinguir   to distinguish

Present Indicative: *distingo*, distingues, etc.   I distinguish, etc.

Imperfect: distinguía, etc.   I was distinguishing, etc.

Preterit: distinguí, etc.   I distinguished, etc.

Future: distinguiré, etc.   I will distinguish, etc.

Conditional: distinguiría, etc.   I would distinguish, etc.

Present Participle: distinguiendo   distinguishing

Past Participle: distinguido   distinguished

Present Subjunctive: *distinga, distingas, distinga, distingamos, distingáis, distingan*   I may distinguish, etc.

Imperfect Subjunctive: distinguiera (distinguiese) etc.   I might distinguish, etc.

Present Perfect Subjunctive: haya distinguido, etc.   I may have distinguished, etc.

Pluperfect Subjunctive: hubiera (hubiese) distinguido, etc.   I might have distinguished, etc.

Others:

extinguir to extinguish	*perseguir* to persecute, pursue;*
seguir to follow;*	*proseguir* to prosecute, pursue*
conseguir to get, obtain;*	* see page 86

Verbs ending in -*quir* change *qu* to *c* before *o* or *a*.

Delinquir   to break the law

Present Indicative: *delinco*, delinques, etc.   I break the law, etc.
Imperfect: delinquía, etc.   I was breaking the law, etc.
Preterit: delinquí, etc.   I broke the law, etc.
Future: delinquiré, etc.   I will break the law, etc.
Conditional: delinquiría, etc.   I would break the law, etc.
Present Participle: delinquiendo   breaking the law
Past Participle: delinquido   broken the law
Present Subjunctive: *delinca, delincas, delinca, delincamos, delincáis, delincan*   I may break the law, etc.
Imperfect Subjunctive:delinquiera (delinquiese), etc.   I might break the law, etc.
Present Perfect Subjunctive: haya delinquido, etc.   I may have broken the law, etc.
Pluperfect Subjunctive: hubiera (hubiese) delinquido, etc.   I might have broken the law, etc.

Para practicar

Write the infinitives in the tense and person indicated:

Present indicative   **yo**

encoger	dirigir	coger	exigir	ejercer	convencer
_____	_____	_____	_____	_____	_____

esparcir	extinguir	delinquir	acoger
_____	_____	_____	_____

Present subjunctive   **nosotros**

extinguir	delinquir	distinguir	escoger	infligir	fingir
_____	_____	_____	_____	_____	_____

coger	esparcir	ejercer	dirigir
_____	_____	_____	_____

Aplicación

Translate into English:

1. ejerzo _____
2. Ud. convenció _____
3. esparciré _____
4. acogías _____
5. ellos distingan _____
6. finjamos _____
7. Uds. han convencido _____
8. dirigiré _____
9. él seguiría _____
10. extingas _____

11. ejercías _____
12. exijo _____
13. seguí _____
14. extinguiste _____
15. ellos convenzan _____
16. fingí _____
17. él delinquió _____
18. ellos cojan _____
19. extingo _____
20. delincáis _____

Mastery Test

Translate into Spanish:

1. you (s., fam.) might conquer _____
2. I may inflict _____
3. I distinguish _____
4. we exercised _____
5. I do not demand _____
6. you (s., fam.) may not distinguish _____
7. he will not convince _____
8. will you (pl., for.) choose? _____
9. let us not extinguish _____
10. I scattered _____

11. we directed _____

12. he distinguished _____

13. I break the law _____

14. you (s., fam.) exercise _____

15. he may welcome _____

16. they may extinguish _____

17. they may not convince _____

18. I pretend _____

19. you (pl., fam.) will distinguish _____

20. you (s., fam.) may not break the law _____

Verbs ending in *-eer* change the *i* to *y* in the third-person singular and plural of the preterit, all persons of the imperfect subjunctive and the present participle.

Creer   to believe

Present Indicative: creo, etc.   I believe, etc.

Imperfect: creía, etc.   I was believing, etc.

Preterit: creí, creíste, *creyó*, creímos, creísteis, *creyeron*   I believed, etc.

Future: creeré, etc.   I will believe, etc.

Conditional: creería, etc.   I would believe, etc.

Present Participle: *creyendo*   believing

Past Participle: creído   believed

Present Subjunctive: crea, etc.   I may believe, etc.

Imperfect Subjunctive: *creyera* (*creyese*), etc.   I might believe, etc.

Present Perfect Subjunctive: haya creído, etc.   I may have believed, etc.

Pluperfect Subjunctive: hubiera (hubiese) creído, etc.   I might have believed, etc.

Additional Note: *-er* and *-ir* verbs whose stems end in a vowel have a written accent on the *i* of the past participle. The past participle of such verbs is otherwise regular. Example: *creer   creído*.

Others:

leer	reír*
poseer	oír*
traer*	huir*
caer*	

* See individual conjugations for these verbs (*traer*, p. 116; *caer*, p. 97; *reír*, pp. 86−87; *oír*, p. 108; *huir*, p. 87).

Most verbs ending in -cer or -cir preceded by a vowel add z before c when followed by o or a.

Conocer   to know, be acquainted with

Present Indicative: *conozco*, conoces, etc.   I know, etc.

Imperfect: conocía, etc.   I was knowing, etc.

Preterit: conocí, etc.   I knew, etc.

Future: conoceré, etc.   I will know, etc.

Conditional: conocería, etc.   I would know, etc.

Present Participle: conociendo   knowing

Past Participle: conocido   known

Present Subjunctive: *conozca, conozcas, conozca, conozcamos, conozcáis, conozcan*   I may know, etc.

Imperfect Subjunctive: conociera (conociese), etc.   I might know, etc.

Present Perfect Subjunctive: haya conocido, etc.   I may have known, etc.

Pluperfect Subjunctive: hubiera (hubiese) conocido, etc.   I might have known, etc.

Others:

agradecer to thank	*desaparecer* to disappear
reconocer to recognize	*enriquecerse* to become rich
desconocer to be unacquainted	*aparecer* to appear
complacer to please	*parecer* to seem
aborrecer to hate	*merecer* to deserve
compadecer to pity	*obedecer* to obey
carecer to lack	*ofrecer* to offer

Some verbs ending in -iar accent the *i* of the stem in all forms of the present indicative and present subjunctive, except the *nosotros* and *vosotros* forms.

Enviar   to send

Present Indicative: *envío, envías, envía*, enviamos, enviáis, *envían*   I send, etc.

Imperfect: enviaba, etc.   I was sending, etc.

Preterit: envié, etc.   I sent, etc.

Future: enviaré, etc.   I will send, etc.

Conditional: enviaría, etc.   I would send, etc.

Present Participle: enviando   sending

Past Participle: enviado   sent

Present Subjunctive: *envíe, envíes, envíe*, enviemos, enviéis, *envíen*   I may send, etc.

Imperfect Subjunctive: enviara (enviase), etc.   I might send, etc.

Present Perfect Subjunctive: haya enviado, etc.   I may have sent, etc.

Pluperfect Subjunctive: hubiera (hubiese) enviado, etc.   I might have sent, etc.

Others:

desafiar   to defy, challenge
confiar   to trust
desconfiar   to mistrust
guiar   to guide

Verbs ending in *-uar* preceded by any consonant except *c* or *g* accent the *u* in all forms of the present indicative and present subjunctive except the *nosotros* and *vosotros* forms.

Continuar   to continue

Present Indicative: continúo, continúas, continúa, continuamos, continuáis, *continúan*   I continue, etc.

Imperfect: continuaba, etc.   I was continuing, etc.

Preterit: continué, etc.   I continued, etc.

Future: continuaré etc.   I will continue, etc.

Conditional: continuaría, etc.   I would continue, etc.

Present Participle: continuando   continuing

Past Participle: continuado   continued

Present Subjunctive: continúe, continúes, continúe, continuemos, continuéis, *continúen*   I may continue, etc.

Imperfect Subjunctive: continuara (continuase), etc.   I might continue, etc.

Present Perfect Subjunctive: haya continuado, etc.   I may have continued, etc.

Pluperfect Subjunctive: hubiera (hubiese) continuado, etc.   I might have continued, etc.

Others:
insinuar   to insinuate
habituarse   to grow accustomed to
descontinuar   to discontinue
graduarse   to graduate, be graduated

Para practicar

Write the infinitives in the tense and person indicated:

Present subjunctive   **tú**

aparecer	ofrecer	merecer	reconocer	compadecer	confiar
___	___	___	___	___	___

guiar	descontinuar
___	___

Present indicative   **yo**

desafiar	parecer	obedecer	agradecer	insinuar	desconfiar
___	___	___	___	___	___

Preterit   **Uds.**

leer	poseer	enviar	continuar	conocer	ofrecer
___	___	___	___	___	___

Aplicación

Change each verb to the corresponding tense in the plural:

1. estoy leyendo _____
2. envías _____
3. continúes _____
4. ofrezco _____
5. Ud. desafíe _____
6. aborrezcas _____
7. yo merezca _____
8. Ud. aparezca _____
9. guío _____
10. desconoció _____

11. poseyó _____
12. Ud. insinúe _____
13. se enriquezca _____
14. parecí _____
15. me habitué _____
16. yo creyese _____
17. Ud. complacía _____
18. ella desconfía _____
19. descontinúo _____
20. reconozco _____

Mastery Test

Translate into Spanish:

1. did she read? _____
2. we may disappear _____
3. he may continue _____
4. they may send _____
5. I was possessing _____
6. you (s., for.) may not know _____
_____

7. we may mistrust _____
8. I do not guide _____
9. you (s., fam.) might read _____
_____
10. he may pity _____
_____
11. I was sending _____

12. you (s., fam.) may discontinue _____

_____

13. we were believing _____

14. you (pl., fam.) disappear _____

_____

15. they sent _____

16. she did not believe _____

17. I hated _____

18. do you (s., fam.) trust? _____

_____

19. they may know _____

20. she continued _____

Orthographic Stem Changes

Verbs ending in -*gar* with stem-vowel *e* or *o* change *g* to *gu* before *e* and also change the stem vowel from *e* to *ie* and *o* to *ue* in all forms of the present indicative and present subjunctive, except the *nosotros* and *vosotros* forms (see pages 62 and 72).

Negar   to deny

Present Indicative: *niego, niegas, niega,* negamos, negáis, *niegan*   I deny, etc.

Preterit: *negué,* negaste, etc.   I denied, etc.

Present Subjunctive: *niegue, niegues, niegue,* neguemos, neguéis, *nieguen*   I may deny, etc.

All other forms are regular.

Others:
cegar   to blind
rogar   to ask, beg

Colgar   to hang up

cuelgo, cuelgas, cuelga, colgamos, colgáis, *cuelgan*   I hang up, etc.

colgué, colgaste, etc.   I hung up, etc.

cuelgue, cuelgues, cuelgue, colguemos, colguéis, cuelguen   I may hang up, etc.

Note one verb that ends in -*gar* and has the stem vowel *u* change to *ue,* in addition to the orthographic change of *g* to *gu:*

Jugar   to play

Present Indicative: *juego, juegas, juega,* jugamos, jugáis, *juegan*   I play, etc.

Preterit: *jugué,* jugaste, etc.   I played, etc.

Present Subjunctive: *juegue, juegues, juegue, juguemos, juguéis, jueguen*   I may play, etc.

All other forms are regular. Jugar is the only verb of this type.

Verbs ending in -*zar* with the stem vowel *e* or *o* change *z* to *c* before *e* and stem vowels *e* to *ie* and *o* to *ue* in all forms of the present indicative and present subjunctive except the *nosotros* and *vosotros* forms (see pages 62 and 73).

Empezar   to begin

Present Indicative: *empiezo, empiezas, empieza,* empezamos, empezáis, *empiezan*   I begin, etc.

Preterit: *empecé,* empezaste, etc.   I began, etc.

Present Subjunctive: *empiece, empieces, empiece,* empecemos, empecéis, *empiecen*   I may begin, etc.

Almorzar   to eat lunch

almuerzo, almuerzas, almuerza, almorzamos, almorzáis, *almuerzan*   I eat lunch, etc.

almorcé, almorzaste, etc.   I ate lunch, etc.

almuerce, almuerces, almuerce, almorcemos, almorcéis, almuercen   I may eat lunch, etc.

All other forms are regular.

Others:
tropezar   to stumble
esforzarse   to try hard

Verbs ending in *-egir* change *g* to *j* before *o* or *a* and stem-vowel *e* to *i* in accordance with rules for stem-changing verbs of Class III (see pages 69 and 77).

Colegir   to collect

Present Indicative: *colijo*, *coliges*, *colige*, colegimos, colegís, *coligen*   I collect, etc.
Preterit: colegí, colegiste, *coligió*, colegimos, colegisteis, *coligieron*   I collected, etc.
Present Participle: *coligiendo*   collecting
Present Subjunctive: *colija*, *colijas*, *colija*, *colijamos*, *colijáis*, *colijan*   I may collect, etc.
Imperfect Subjunctive: *coligiera* (*coligiese*), *coligieras*, *coligiera*, *coligieramos*, *coligierais*, *coligieran*   I
                        might collect, etc.

Others:
corregir   to correct
elegir   to elect

Verbs ending in *-eguir* change *gu* to *g* before *o* or *a* and *e* to *i* in accordance with rules for stem-changing verbs of Class III.

Seguir   to follow

Present Indicative: *sigo*, *sigues*, *sigue*, seguimos, seguís, *siguen*   I follow, etc.
Preterit: seguí, seguiste, *siguió*, seguimos, seguisteis, *siguieron*   I followed, etc.
Present Participle: *siguiendo*   following
Present Subjunctive: *siga*, *sigas*, *siga*, *sigamos*, *sigáis*, *sigan*   I may follow, etc.
Imperfect Subjunctive: *siguiera* (siguiese), etc.   I might follow, etc.

Stem has *i* throughout imperfect subjunctive.

Others:
conseguir   to get, obtain
perseguir   to persecute, pursue
proseguir   to prosecute, pursue

Verbs ending in *-eír* change *e* to *i* in accordance with rules of stem-changing verbs of Class III. In addition, when the stem is stressed, the *i* has a written accent. When the stem is not changed and is followed by a stressed *i* in the ending, the *i* requires a written accent, as does the infinitive.

Reír   to laugh

Present Indicative: *río*, *ríes*, *ríe*, reímos, reís, *ríen*   I laugh, etc.
Preterit: reí, reíste, *rió*, reímos, reísteis, *rieron*   I laughed, etc.
Present Participle: *riendo*   laughing

Past Participle: reído
Present Subjunctive: *ría, rías, ría, riamos, riáis, rían* I may laugh, etc.
Imperfect Subjunctive: *riera* (*riese*) etc. I might laugh, etc.

Others:
sonreír to smile

Verbs ending in *-uir* insert *y* before all endings after an accented stem and change unaccented *i* to *y* before *e* or *a* in endings (see page 80).

Huir to flee

Present Indicative: *huyo, huyes, huye,* huímos, huís, *huyen* I flee, etc.
Preterit: huí, huiste, *huyó,* huimos, huisteis, *huyeron* I fled, etc.
Present Participle: *huyendo* fleeing
Present Subjunctive: *huya, huyas, huya, huyamos, huyáis, huyan* I may flee, etc.
Imperfect Subjunctive: *huyera* (*huyese*), etc. I might flee, etc.

Others:

concluir to conclude	*incluir* to include
destruir to destroy	*restituir* to restore
instruir to instruct	*constituir* to constitute, consist
construir to construct	

Para practicar

Write the infinitives in the tense and person indicated:

Present indicative **yo**

corregir	rogar	cegar	tropezar	conseguir	construir
_____	_____	_____	_____	_____	_____

sonreír

_____

Present indicative   **Ud.**

negar	perseguir	reír	destruir	esforzarse	elegir
_____	_____	_____	_____	_____	_____

jugar

_____

Preterit   **yo**

colegir	rogar	almorzar	incluir	reír	proseguir
_____	_____	_____	_____	_____	_____

cegar

_____

Preterit   **ellos**

corregir	conseguir	sonreír	restituir	elegir	instruir
_____	_____	_____	_____	_____	_____

negar

_____

Present subjunctive   **tú**

cegar	jugar	tropezar	corregir	proseguir	destruir
_____	_____	_____	_____	_____	_____

reír

_____

Present subjunctive   **nosotros**

negar	esforzarse	elegir	conseguir	sonreír	concluir
_____	_____	_____	_____	_____	_____

jugar

_____

Imperfect subjunctive **él**

corregir	proseguir	reír	construir	elegir	constituir
_____	_____	_____	_____	_____	_____

conseguir

_____

Present participle

colegir	colgar	almorzar	sonreír	destruir	perseguir
_____	_____	_____	_____	_____	_____

incluir

_____

Past participle

cegar	empezar	elegir	seguir	reír	concluir
_____	_____	_____	_____	_____	_____

huir

_____

Aplicación

Change from singular to plural in the same tense:

1. ruegue Ud. _____
2. tropiezo _____
3. él almuerce _____
4. cegué _____
5. escojo _____
6. empecé _____
7. juega _____
8. me esforcé _____

9. cuelgues _____
10. empiezo _____
11. huye _____
12. Ud. sonrió _____
13. él destruyó _____
14. yo concluyese _____
15. has huido _____
16. él corrija _____

17. Ud. consiguió _____   24. persigue _____

18. sigo _____   25. incluyas _____

19. yo escogiera _____   26. yo concluía _____

20. consigas _____   27. Ud. había reído _____

21. él estaba siguiendo _____   28. instruyo _____

22. yo elija _____   29. Ud. ha restituido _____

23. corrijo _____   30. está sonriendo _____

Mastery Test
Orthographic changes and orthographic-stem changes:

A. Write in English:

1. yo apague _____

2. ejerzo _____

3. envías _____

4. tropiezo _____

5. ¡extinga Ud.! _____

6. ofrezco _____

7. entregué _____

8. ellos distingan _____

9. desconozcas _____

10. jugué _____

11. finjamos _____

12. guío _____

13. Ud. almuerce _____

14. corrijo _____

15. él poseyó _____

B. Write in Spanish:

1. I paid _____

2. I might choose _____

3. did she read? _____

4. I did not find out _____

5. they followed _____

6. he may continue _____

7. he may not place _____

8. you (s., fam.) may not extinguish _____

_____

9. they may send _____

10. we may arrive _____

11. did you (s., for.) obtain? _____

_____

12. you (s., fam.) may not know _____

_____

16. repliques _____

17. ellos cojan _____

18. Ud. insinúe _____

19. amenaces _____

20. exijo _____

21. yo creyese _____

22. marqué _____

23. consigas _____

24. sonrío _____

25. Ud. ruegue _____

26. ellos convenzan _____

27. Ud. concluyese _____

28. Uds. apacigüen _____

29. delincáis _____

30. destruyó _____

13. you (s., for.) may cross _____
_____

14. I follow _____

15. I don't guide _____

16. I begged _____

17. I break the law _____

18. you (s., fam.) might read _____
_____

19. you (pl., fam.) may begin _____
_____

20. he may direct _____

21. they destroyed _____

22. I did not explain _____

23. I pretend _____

24. you (s., fam.) do not laugh _____
_____

25. you (s., for.) may reply _____
_____

26. they may not convince _____
_____

27. we were believing _____

28. I threw _____

29. you (s., fam.) may choose _____
_____

30. we might conclude _____

Repaso general 1

A. Change each verb from singular to plural in the same tense:

1. parto _____

2. comprendiste _____

3. él vivía _____

4. asistiré _____

5. tomarías _____

6. estoy escribiendo _____

7. estaba vistiéndose _____

8. he hablado _____

9. Ud. había vendido _____

10. habrás asistido _____

11. él habría bebido _____

12. conteste Ud. _____

13. aprendieras _____

14. él haya entrado _____

15. yo hubiera tomado _____

16. acuerdo _____

17. se acueste _____

18. yo consienta _____

19. no se divierte _____

20. Ud. pidió _____

21. leyó _____

22. río _____

23. negué _____

B. Write in Spanish:

1. they fear _____

2. you (s., fam.) used to drink _____
   _____

3. you (pl., fam.) may show _____
   _____

4. I began _____

5. did you (s., fam.) speak? _____
   _____

6. they served _____

7. we were believing _____

8. you (pl., fam.) might read _____
   _____

9. he would not write _____

10. he notices _____

11. they may not convince _____
    _____

12. he may not begin _____

13. you (s., fam.) were speaking _____
    _____

14. it is snowing _____

15. you (pl., for.) may explain _____
    _____

16. you (pl., fam.) may direct _____

24. Ud. incluya _____

_____

25. juegues _____

17. I will have taught _____

26. reconozco _____

18. they might ask for _____

27. Ud. persiguió _____

19. you (s., fam.) do not laugh _____

28. almuerces _____

_____

29. averigüe _____

20. I do not guide _____

30. distingo _____

21. let us fear _____

22. I choose _____

23. do you (s., fam.) continue? _____

_____

24. I did not explain _____

25. he was selling _____

26. I begged _____

27. they destroyed _____

28. you (s., fam.) may choose _____

_____

29. they used to carry _____

30. he sends _____

Repaso general 2

A. Make each simple tense into a compound one in the same person:

B. Write in Spanish:

1. temía _____

1. they would have left _____

2. parto _____

2. they may read _____

3. vivían _____

3. we might conclude _____

4. necesitaré _____

4. she is not studying _____

A. Make each simple tense into a compound one in the same person: (*continued*)

5. partiríamos _____

6. comas _____

7. vendiésemos _____

8. Ud. rió _____

9. restituyes _____

10. envían _____

11. descontinúo _____

12. obedezco _____

13. creyó _____

14. desaparezcan _____

15. yo poseyera _____

16. tropieza _____

17. distinga Ud. _____

18. juegan _____

19. expliquen _____

20. consigo _____

21. hirió _____

22. eliges _____

23. él delinca _____

24. sonríen _____

25. destruyeron _____

26. hablaréis _____

27. aprendí _____

B. Write in Spanish: (*continued*)

5. they understand _____

6. I paid _____

7. you (s., fam.) may cross _____

_____

8. you (s., for.) would carry _____

_____

9. we may close _____

10. I might choose _____

11. did you (s., fam.) obtain? _____

_____

12. we might not attend _____

13. you (pl., fam.) might prevent _____

_____

14. did she read? _____

15. let us arrive _____

16. do you (s., for.) open? _____

_____

17. they prevented _____

18. I did not find out _____

19. you (pl., fam.) do not cross _____

_____

20. you (s., fam.) will enter _____

_____

28. durmió _____

29. corrigiéramos _____

30. huyera _____

21. I dress myself _____

22. they followed _____

23. I close _____

24. would you (pl., for.) read? _____
_____

25. they may die _____

26. continue! (pl., for.) _____

27. I follow _____

28. you (pl., for.) will have lived _____
_____

29. you (pl., fam.) may lose _____
_____

30. he may not look for _____

Irregular Verbs

Andar   to walk

Present Indicative: ando, andas, etc.   I walk, etc.

Imperfect: andaba, etc.   I was walking, etc.

Preterit: *anduve, anduviste, anduvo, anduvimos, anduvisteis, anduvieron*   I walked, etc.

Future: andaré, etc.   I will walk, etc.

Conditional: andaría, etc.   I would walk, etc.

Present Participle: andando   walking

Past Participle: andado   walked

Present Subjunctive: ande, etc.   I may walk, etc.

Imperfect Subjunctive: *anduviera (anduviese) anduvieras, anduviera, anduviéramos, anduvierais, anduvieran*   I might walk, etc.

Present Perfect Subjunctive: haya andado, etc.   I may have walked, etc.

Pluperfect Subjunctive: hubiera (hubiese) andado, etc.   I might have walked, etc

Asir   to seize

Present Indicative: *asgo*, ases, etc.   I seize, etc.

Imperfect: asía, etc.   I was seizing, etc.

Preterit: así, asiste, etc.   I seized, etc.

Future: asiré, etc.   I will seize, etc.

Conditonal: asiría, etc.   I would seize, etc.

Present Participle: asiendo   seizing

Past Participle: asido   seized

Present Subjunctive: *asga, asgas, asga, asgamos, asgáis, asgan*   I may seize, etc.

Imperfect Subjunctive: asiera (asiese), etc.   I might seize, etc.

Present Perfect Subjunctive: haya asido, etc.   I may have seized, etc.

Pluperfect Subjunctive: hubiera (hubiese) asido, etc.   I might have seized, etc.

Other:
desasir   to loosen

Caber   to be room for, to fit

Present Indicative: *quepo*, cabes, etc.   I fit, etc.

Imperfect: cabía, etc.   I was fitting, etc.

Preterit: *cupe, cupiste, cupo, cupimos, cupisteis, cupieron*   I fitted, etc.

Future: *cabré, cabrás, cabrá, cabremos, cabréis, cabrán*   I will fit, etc.

Conditional: *cabría*, etc.   I would fit, etc.

Present Participle: cabiendo   fitting

Past Participle: cabido   fitted

Present Subjunctive: *quepa, quepas, quepa, quepamos, quepáis, quepan*   I may fit, etc.

Imperfect Subjunctive: *cupiera (cupiese)*, etc.   I might fit, etc.

Present Perfect Subjunctive: haya cabido, etc.   I may have fitted, etc.

Pluperfect Subjunctive: hubiera (hubiese) cabido, etc.   I might have fitted, etc.

Caer   to fall

Present Indicative: *caigo*, caes, cae, caemos, caéis, caen   I fall, etc.

Imperfect: caía, etc.   I was falling, etc.

Preterit: caí, caíste, *cayó*, caímos, caísteis, *cayeron*   I fell, etc.

Future: caeré, etc.   I will fall, etc.

Conditional: caería, etc.   I would fall, etc.

Present Participle: *cayendo*   falling

Past Participle: caído   fallen

Present Subjunctive: *caiga, caigas, caiga, caigamos, caigáis, caigan*   I may fall, etc.

Imperfect Subjunctive: *cayera, (cayese)*, etc.   I might fall, etc.

Present Perfect Subjunctive: haya caído, etc.   I may have fallen, etc.

Pluperfect Subjunctive: hubiera (hubiese) caído, etc.   I might have fallen, etc.

Others:

decaer   to decline, decay, fade

Para practicar

Write the infinitives in the tense and person indicated:

Present indicative   **yo**

desasir	caber	andar	decaer
_____	_____	_____	_____

Uds.

asir	andar	caer	caber
_____	_____	_____	_____

Preterit   **él**

desasir	caber	andar	caer
_____	_____	_____	_____

Future   **nosotros**

asir	decaer	caber	andar
_____	_____	_____	_____

Present subjunctive **tú**

desasir	caer	caber	andar
_____	_____	_____	_____

Imperfect subjunctive **vosotros**

decaer	andar	caber	asir
_____	_____	_____	_____

Aplicación

Translate into English:

1. ellos caerían _____

2. cabremos _____

3. hayas caído _____

4. andabais _____

5. Uds. cabrían _____

6. ellos cayeron _____

7. decaeríais _____

8. cupiste _____

9. desasimos _____

10. anduvimos _____

11. decaigamos _____

12. ellos quepan _____

13. Uds. caigan _____

14. asiré _____

15. decaímos _____

16. él caerá _____

17. yo cupiera _____

18. caigo _____

19. quepo _____

20. ellos asgan _____

21. decayeras _____

22. andaremos _____

23. ellos hubieran asido _____

24. ellos habrían andado _____

25. Uds. desasirán _____

26. ellos están decayendo _____

27. andemos _____

28. él habrá decaído _____

29. ellos anduviesen _____

30. Uds. asen _____

Mastery Test

Write in Spanish:

1. they would not fall _____

2. I might have walked _____

3. they would seize _____

4. were you (s., fam.) walking? _____

_____

5. they are fading _____

6. they might loosen _____

7. you (pl., fam.) would decline _____

_____

8. will I walk? _____

9. I loosen _____

10. he walked _____

11. did he fit? _____

12. we were loosening _____

13. they declined _____

14. we should have fitted _____

_____

15. I shall not fall _____

16. he fits _____

17. we might walk _____

18. he had seized _____

19. he would not have fallen _____

_____

20. he may walk _____

21. you (s., fam.) had seized _____

_____

22. I walk _____

23. you (pl., for.) would fall _____

_____

24. did he seize? _____

25. he has fallen _____

26. we may fit _____

27. you (s., fam.) used to walk _____

_____

28. we were falling _____

29. you (s., fam.) may have walked _____

_____

30. we had fitted _____

31. I may have seized _____

32. you (pl., fam.) fell _____

33. I might have fallen _____

34. you (s., for.) fitted _____

35. I might fit _____

36. you (s., fam.) decline _____

37. they may seize _____

38. we might fall _____

39. I may not fit _____

40. you (pl., fam.) may fall _____

_____

Conducir   to lead, conduct

Present Indicative: *conduzco*, conduces, etc.   I lead, etc.

Imperfect: conducía, etc.   I was leading, etc.

Preterit: *conduje, condujiste, condujo, condujimos, condujisteis, condujeron*   I led, etc.

Future: conduciré, etc.   I will lead, etc.

Conditional: conduciría, etc.   I would lead, etc.

Present Participle: conduciendo   leading

Past Participle: conducido   led

Present Subjunctive: *conduzca, conduzcas, conduzca, conduzcamos, conduzcáis, conduzcan*   I may lead, etc.

Imperfect Subjunctive: *condujera* (*condujese*), etc.   I might lead, etc.

Present Perfect Subjunctive: haya conducido, etc.   I may have led, etc.

Pluperfect Subjunctive: hubiera (hubiese) conducido, etc.   I might have led, etc.

Others:
deducir   to deduce
traducir   to translate
producir   to produce

Dar   to give

Present Indicative: *doy*, das, da, damos, *dais*, dan   I give, etc.

Imperfect: daba, etc.   I was giving, etc.

Preterit: *di, diste, dio, dimos, disteis, dieron*   I gave, etc.

Future   daré, etc.   I will gave, etc.

Conditional: daría, etc.   I would give, etc.

Present Participle: dando   giving

Past Participle: dado   given

Present Sujunctive: *dé, des, dé, demos, deis, den*   I may give, etc.

Imperfect Subjunctive: *diera*, (*diese*), etc.   I might give, etc.

Present Perfect Subjunctive: haya dado, etc.   I may have given, etc.

Pluperfect Subjunctive: hubiera (hubiese) dado, etc.   I might have given, etc.

Decir   to say, tell

Present Indicative: *digo, dices, dice*, decimos, decís, *dicen*   to say, etc.

Imperfect: decía, etc.   I was saying, etc.

Preterit: *dije, dijiste, dijo,* dijimos, dijisteis, dijeron   I said, etc.

Future: *diré, dirás, dirá, diremos, diréis, dirán*   I will tell, etc.

Conditional: *diría*, etc.   I would tell, etc.

Present Participle: *diciendo*   saying

Past Participle: *dicho*   said

Present Subjunctive: *diga, digas, diga, digamos, digáis, digan*   I may tell, etc.

Imperfect Subjunctive: *dijera* (*dijese*), etc.   I might say, etc.

Present Perfect Subjunctive: haya *dicho*, etc.   I may have said, etc.

Pluperfect Subjunctive: hubiera (hubiese) *dicho*, etc.   I might have said, etc.

Others:
maldecir   to curse
bendecir   to bless*

* Note that *maldecir* and *bendecir* are regular in the future and the conditional (*maldeciré, bendeciría*, etc.). The past participles of these verbs are also regular (*maldecido, bendecido*).

Errar   to err, to wander

Pesent Indicative: *yerro, yerras, yerra*, erramos, erráis, *yerran*   I wander, etc.

Imperfect: erraba, etc.   I was wandering, etc.

Preterit: erré, etc.   I wandered, etc.

Future: erraré, etc.   I will wander, etc.

Conditional: erraría, etc.   I would wander, etc.

Present participle: errando   wandering

Past Participle: errado   wandered

Present Subjunctive: *yerre, yerres, yerre*, erremos, erréis, *yerren*   I may wander, etc.

Imperfect Subjunctive: errara (errase), etc.   I might wander, etc.

Present Perfect Subjunctive: haya errado, etc.   I may have wandered, etc.

Pluperfect Subjunctive: hubiera (hubiese) errado, etc.   I might have wandered, etc.

Para practicar

Write the infinitives in the person and tense indicated:

Present indicative **yo**

deducir   maldecir   errar   dar   traducir

_____   _____   _____   _____   _____

Preterit **ellos**

producir	bendecir	dar	conducir	errar
_____	_____	___	_____	_____

Future **Ud.**

traducir	maldecir	deducir	bendecir	dar
_____	_____	_____	_____	___

Pluperfect indicative **Uds.**

dar	deducir	bendecir	errar	decir
___	_____	_____	_____	_____

Present subjunctive **tú**

dar	producir	bendecir	errar	decir
___	_____	_____	_____	_____

Imperfect subjunctive **nosotros**

errar	traducir	maldecir	dar	conducir
_____	_____	_____	___	_____

Aplicación

Write in English:

1. dedujisteis _____

2. das _____

3. él dirá _____

4. erremos _____

5. conducíamos _____

6. ellos den _____

7. digamos _____

8. maldecías _____

9. él traduce _____

10. Ud. habría dado _____

11. ellos dijeron _____

12. yo haya dicho _____

13. ella condujo _____

14. doy _____

15. yerres _____

16. diríamos _____

17. yo deduzca _____

18. Ud. dio _____

19. ellos bendicen _____

20. Uds. yerran _____

21. él produciría _____

22. dieras _____

23. él dijera _____

24. yerro _____

25. ella tradujera _____

26. dábamos _____

27. ellos habrían maldicho _____

_____

28. erré _____

29. produzco _____

30. daré _____

Mastery Test

Write in Spanish:

1. you (s., fam.) will say _____

_____

2. you (pl., fam.) lead _____

3. let us wander _____

4. I may have told _____

5. he was not giving _____

6. you (s., fam.) translated _____

_____

7. he might bless _____

8. we will give _____

9. you (pl., for.) may produce _____

10. did he lead? _____

11. you (pl., fam.) might not say _____

_____

12. does he give? _____

13. I do wander _____

14. he might deduce _____

15. we would curse _____

16. they gave _____

17. I might produce _____

18. do not translate! (pl., for.) _____

19. are they saying? _____

20. they wandered _____

21. they might have given _____

_____

22. have you (pl., fam.) not told? _____

_____

23. I produce _____

24. he wanders _____

25. we will not tell _____

26. they were not saying _____

27. I do not give _____

28. I may deduce _____

29. they may not translate _____

_____

30. you (s., fam.) cursed _____

31. did you (pl., fam.) give? _____

_____

32. we will lead _____

33. you (s., for.) may give _____

_____

34. I bless _____

35. they produced _____

36. you (s., fam.) were translating _____

_____

37. he might not give _____

38. he may curse _____

39. they may have given _____

40. he may not lead _____

Estar   to be (in a state or condition)

Present Indicative: *estoy, estás, está*, estamos, estáis, *están*   I am, etc.

Imperfect: estaba, etc.   I was, etc.

Preterit: *estuve, estuviste, estuvo, estuvimos, estuvisteis, estuvieron*   I was, etc.

Future: estaré, etc.   I will be, etc.

Conditional: estaría, etc.   I would be, etc.

Present Participle: estando   being

Past Participle: estado   been

Present Subjunctive: *esté, estés, esté*, estemos, estéis, *estén*   I may be, etc.

Imperfect Subjunctive: *estuviera* (*estuviese*), etc.   I might be, etc.

Present Perfect Subjunctive: haya estado, etc.   I may have been, etc.

Pluperfect Subjunctive: hubiera (hubiese) estado, etc.   I might have been, etc.

Haber   to have (used only as an auxiliary with perfect tenses or in idiomatic expressions. Some tenses are defective, i.e., they do not have complete forms)

Present Indicative: *he, has, ha, hemos*, habéis, *han*   I have, etc.; *hay*   there is, are

Imperfect: había, etc.   I had, etc.; había   there was, were

Preterit: *hube*, hubiste, *hubo, hubimos, hubisteis, hubieron*   I had, etc.; *hubo*   there was, were

Future: habré, habrás, habrá, habremos, habréis, habrán.   I will have, etc.; *habrá*   there will be

Conditional: *habría*, etc.   I would have, etc.; *habría*   there would be

Present Participle: habiendo   having, there being

Past Participle: habido   ha (había, habrá, habría) habido   there has (had, will have, would have) been

Present Subjunctive: *haya, hayas, haya, hayamos, hayáis, hayan*   I may have, etc. *haya*   there may be

Imperfect Subjunctive: hubiera (*hubiese*), etc.   I might have, etc.; *hubiera* (*hubiese*) there might be
Present Perfect Subjunctive: haya habido   there may have been
Pluperfect Subjunctive: hubiera (hubiese) habido   there might have been

Hacer   to do, make

Present Indicative: *hago*, haces, hace, hacemos, hacéis, hacen   I do, etc.
Imperfect: hacía, etc.   I was doing, etc.
Preterit: *hice, hiciste, hizo, hicimos, hicisteis, hicieron*   I did, etc.
Future: *haré, harás, hará haremos, haréis, harán*   I will do, etc.
Conditional: *haría*, etc.   I would do, etc.
Present Participle: haciendo   doing
Past Participle: hecho   done
Present Subjunctive: haga, hagas, haga, hagamos, hagáis, hagan   I may do, etc.
Imperfect Subjunctive: hiciera (*hiciese*), etc.   I might do, etc.
Present Perfect Subjunctive: haya *hecho*, etc.   I may have done, etc.
Pluperfect Subjunctive: hubiera (hubiese) *hecho*, etc.   I might have done, etc.

Other:
satisfacer   to satisfy

Ir   to go

Present Indicative: voy, vas, va, vamos, vais, van   I go, etc.
Imperfect: iba, ibas, iba, íbamos, ibais, iban   I was going, etc.
Preterit: fui, fuiste, fue, fuimos, fuisteis, fueron   I went, etc.
Future: iré, etc.   I will go, etc.
Conditional: iría, etc.   I would go, etc.
Present Participle: yendo   going
Past Participle: ido   gone
Present Subjunctive: vaya, vayas, vaya, vayamos, vayáis, vayan   I may go, etc.
Imperfect Subjunctive: fuera (fuese), etc.   I might go, etc.
Present Perfect Subjunctive: haya ido, etc.   I may have gone, etc.
Pluperfect Subjunctive: hubiera (hubiese) ido, etc.   I might have gone, etc.

Para practicar

Change to the plural of the same tense:

1. voy _____

2. Ud. satisfaga _____

3. habrá _____

4. estoy _____

5. ibas _____

6. yo hubiera _____

7. he _____

8. estuvo _____

9. fui _____

10. hará _____

11. hubiste _____

12. hicieras _____

13. él vaya _____

14. estuvieras _____

15. has hecho _____

16. Ud. haya _____

17. fueras _____

18. satisfizo _____

19. Ud. esté _____

20. satisfago _____

Aplicación

Translate into English:

1. él habrá satisfecho _____

2. estamos _____

3. hay _____

4. fuiste _____

5. él haría _____

6. satisficiste _____

7. habría habido _____

8. hayas hecho _____

9. yo no estaría _____

10. satisfaré _____

11. ellos habían _____

12. hacíamos _____

13. ibais _____

14. satisficiésemos _____

15. haya habido _____

16. yo habría estado _____

17. Ud. satisfaga _____

18. estuvieras _____

19. habrías _____

20. hicimos _____

21. ellos estaban _____

22. él hiciera _____

23. él ha _____

24. no vayas _____

25. yo habría hecho _____

26. satisfacías _____

27. fuéramos _____

28. estén _____

29. estuve _____

30. va _____

Mastery Test

Write in Spanish:

1. we might have gone _____

2. I was (pret) _____

3. I may have done _____

4. they would have satisfied _____

_____

5. he was (imperfect) _____

6. they will not have gone _____

_____

7. we were not doing _____

8. you (pl., for.) will satisfy _____

_____

9. we are _____

10. I had done _____

11. he was going _____

12. I satisfied _____

13. we may be _____

14. there are not _____

15. we do not satisfy _____

16. does she go? _____

17. you (s., for.) will be _____

18. they did _____

19. we may satisfy _____

20. I might not be _____

21. there would have been _____

_____

22. you (s., fam.) might go _____

_____

23. he was satisfying _____

24. there will be _____

25. I may go _____

26. there might have been _____

_____

27. he may satisfy _____

28. you (s., fam.) will do _____

_____

29. there might be _____

30. they might have been _____

_____

31. you (pl., fam.) went _____

32. there has been _____

33. they may not do _____

34. I satisfy _____

35. they might have done _____

36. I will not go _____

37. there may be _____

38. we would do _____

39. there was (imperfect) _____

40. I am not _____

Oír to hear

Present Indicative: *oigo, oyes, oye,* oímos, oís, *oyen*   I hear, etc.

Imperfect: oía, oías, etc.   I was hearing, etc.

Preterit: oí, oíste, *oyó,* oímos, oísteis, *oyeron*   I heard, etc.

Future: oiré, etc.   I will hear, etc.

Conditional: oiría, etc.   I would hear, etc.

Present Participle: *oyendo*   hearing

Past Participle: oído   heard

Present Subjunctive: *oiga, oigas, oiga, oigamos, oigáis, oigan*   I may hear, etc.

Imperfect Subjunctive: *oyera* (*oyese*), etc.   I might hear, etc.

Present Perfect Subjunctive: haya oído, etc.   I may have heard, etc.

Pluperfect Subjunctive: hubiera (hubiese) oído, etc.   I might have heard, etc.

Oler to smell

Present Indicative: *huelo, hueles, huele,* olemos, oléis, *huelen*   I smell, etc.

Imperfect: olía, etc.   I was smelling, etc.

Preterit: olí, oliste, etc.   I smelled, etc.

Future: oleré, etc.   I will smell, etc.

Conditional: olería, etc.   I would smell, etc.

Present Participle: oliendo   smelling

Past Participle: olido   smelled

Present Subjunctive: *huela, huelas, huela,* olamos, oláis, *huelan*   I may smell, etc.

Imperfect Subjunctive: oliera (oliese), etc.   I might smell, etc.

Present Perfect Subjunctive: haya olido, etc.   I may have smelled, etc.

Pluperfect Subjunctive: hubiera (hubiese) olido, etc.   I might have smelled, etc.

Poder to be able

Present Indicative: *puedo puedes, puede,* podemos, podéis, *pueden,*   I can, am able, etc.

Imperfect: podía, etc.   I was able, could, etc.

Preterit: pude, pudiste, pudo, pudimos, pudisteis, pudieron   I was able, could etc.

Future: podré, podrás, podra, podremos, podréis, podrán   I will be able, etc.

Conditional: podría, etc.   I would be able, could etc.

Present Participle: pudiendo   being able

Past Participle: podido   been able
Present Subjunctive: *pueda, puedas, pueda*, podamos, podáis, *puedan*   I may be able, etc.
Imperfect Subjunctive: *pudiera* (*pudiese*), etc.   I might be able, etc.
Present Perfect Subjunctive: haya podido, etc.   I may have been able, etc.
Pluperfect Subjunctive: hubiera (hubiese) podido, etc.   I might have been able, etc.

Poner   to put, place
Present Indicative: *pongo*, pones, pone, ponemos, ponéis, ponen   I put, etc.
Imperfect: ponía, etc.   I was putting, etc.
Preterit: puse, *pusiste, puso, pusimos, pusisteis, pusieron*   I put, did put, etc.
Future: pondré, *pondrás, pondrá, pondremos, pondréis, pondrán*   I will put, etc.
Conditional: pondría, etc.   I would put, etc.
Present Participle: poniendo   putting
Past Participle: *puesto*   put
Present Subjunctive: *ponga, pongas, ponga, pongamos, pongáis, pongan*   I may put, etc.
Imperfect Subjunctive: *pusiera* (*pusiese*), etc.   I might put, etc.
Present Perfect Subjunctive: haya *puesto*, etc.   I may have put, etc.
Pluperfect Subjunctive: hubiera (hubiese) *puesto*, etc.   I might have put, etc.

Others:
disponer to dispose	*imponer* to impose
exponer to expose	*proponer* to propose
componer to compose	*suponer* to suppose

Para practicar

Change the infinitives to the tense and person indicated:

Present indicative **tú**

proponer	oler	poder	oír	componer
_____	_____	_____	_____	_____

Preterit **Uds.**

disponer	poder	oír	imponer	suponer
_____	_____	_____	_____	_____

Future **yo**

disponer	exponer	imponer	proponer	suponer
_____	_____	_____	_____	_____

Present subjunctive **él**

componer	poder	oír	oler	exponer
_____	_____	_____	_____	_____

Present perfect subjunctive **nosotros**

oír	disponer	poner	suponer	poder
_____	_____	_____	_____	_____

Aplicación

Change the singular verb to plural, retaining the same tense:

1. él pusiera _____

2. yo pueda _____

3. él oiría _____

4. pudiste _____

5. dispones _____

6. yo oía _____

7. Ud. podrá _____

8. olió _____

9. he compuesto _____

10. habré podido _____

11. oiré _____

12. olerías _____

13. él impondría _____

14. él podía _____

15. habrá oído _____

16. huele _____

17. yo exponga _____

18. oyó _____

19. yo pudiera _____

20. yo haya propuesto _____

21. podrías _____

22. oigas _____

23. huelo _____

24. supondrás _____

25. puedes _____

26. Ud. oye _____

27. huelas _____

28. dispuso _____

29. yo oliera _____

30. hubieras puesto _____

Mastery Test

Write in Spanish:

1. you (s., fam.) heard _____

_____

2. we had not been able _____

_____

3. it may smell _____

4. I would not have put _____

5. you (pl., fam.) were not hearing _____

_____

6. they are imposing _____

7. I was able _____

8. does he smell? _____

9. they would hear _____

10. he may be able _____

11. I will have composed _____

_____

12. does she put? _____

13. does he hear? _____

14. you (s., fam.) will not expose _____

_____

15. they may propose _____

16. I might not be able _____

17. we might have heard _____

18. you (pl., for.) would be able _____

_____

19. they might smell _____

20. we may suppose _____

21. you (pl., fam.) will not hear _____

_____

22. are you (s., fam.) able? _____

_____

23. we might dispose _____

24. they will not put _____

25. they heard _____

26. you (pl., fam.) were able (pret) _____

_____

27. she was supposing _____

28. you (s., fam.) will be able _____

_____

29. we might not hear _____

30. did you (pl., fam.) expose? _____

_____

Querer to want, wish, love

Present Indicative: *quiero, quieres, quiere,* queremos, queréis, *quieren* I want, etc.

Imperfect: quería, etc. I was wishing, etc.

Preterit: *quise, quisiste, quiso, quisimos, quisisteis, quisieron* I wanted, etc.

Future: *querré, querrás, querrá, querremos, querréis, querrán* I shall want, etc.

Conditional: *querría,* etc. I would wish, etc.

Present Participle: queriendo wanting

Past Participle: querido wanted

Present Subjunctive: *quiera, quieras, quiera,* queramos, queráis, *quieran* I may want etc.

Imperfect Subjunctive: *quisiera (quisiese),* etc. I might want, etc.

Present Perfect Subjunctive: haya querido, etc. I may have wished, etc.

Pluperfect Subjunctive: hubiera (hubiese) querido, etc. I might have wished, etc.

Saber to know (a fact)

Present Indicative: *sé,* sabes, sabe, sabemos, sabéis, saben I know, etc.

Imperfect: sabía, etc. I was knowing, etc.

Preterit: *supe, supiste, supo, supimos, supisteis, supieron,* I knew, found out, etc.

Future: *sabré, sabrás, sabrá, sabremos, sabréis, sabrán.* I will know, etc.

Conditional: *sabría,* etc. I would know, etc.

Present Participle: sabiendo knowing

Past Participle: sabido known

Present Subjunctive: *sepa, sepas, sepa, sepamos, sepáis, sepan* I may know, etc.

Imperfect Subjunctive: *supiera (supiese),* etc. I might know, etc.

Present Perfect Subjunctive: haya sabido, etc. I may have known, etc.

Pluperfect Subjunctive: hubiera (hubiese) sabido, etc. I might have known, etc.

Salir to go out, leave

Present Indicative: *salgo,* sales, sale, salimos, salís, salen I go out, etc.

Imperfect: salía, etc. I was going out, etc.

Preterit: salí, etc. I went out, etc.

Future: *saldré, saldrás, saldrá, saldremos, saldréis, saldrán* I will go out, etc.

Conditional: *saldría,* etc. I would go out, etc.

Present Participle: saliendo going out

Past Participle: salido gone out

Present Subjunctive: *salga, salgas, salga, salgamos, salgáis, salgan* I may go out, etc.

Imperfect Subjunctive: *saliera (saliese),* etc. I might go out, etc.

Present Perfect Subjunctive: haya salido, etc. I may have gone out, etc.

Pluperfect Subjunctive: hubiera (hubiese) salido, etc. I might have gone out, etc.

Ser to be

Present Indicative: soy, eres, es, somos, sois, son I am, etc.

Imperfect: era, eras, era, éramos, erais, eran I was, etc.

Preterit: fui, fuiste, fue, fuimos, fuisteis, fueron I was, etc.

Future: seré, etc. I will be, etc.

Conditional: sería, etc. I would be, etc.

Present Participle: siendo being

Past Participle: sido been

Present Subjunctive: sea, seas, sea, seamos, seáis, sean I may be, etc.

Imperfect Subjunctive: fuera (fuese), etc. I might be, etc.

Present Perfect Subjunctive: haya sido, etc. I may have been, etc.

Pluperfect Subjuctive: hubiera (hubiese) sido, etc. I might have been, etc.

Note: The preterits of *ser* and *ir* are identical. The context makes clear which one is intended.

Aplicación

A. Change each verb to express past time in the same person.

1. somos _____

2. sepas _____

3. salimos _____

4. sabe _____

5. eres _____

6. salga _____

7. él sea _____

8. soy _____

9. queremos _____

10. salgo _____

11. he sabido _____

12. habéis salido _____

13. quiere _____

B. Change each singular verb to plural in the same tense.

1. yo salía _____

2. Ud. sabrá _____

3. tú querrás _____

4. salió _____

5. sepas _____

6. saldrías _____

7. sabe _____

8. eres _____

9. yo había querido _____

10. salga _____

11. será _____

12. él quisiera _____

13. saldré _____

Aplicación (*cont.*)

14. estás saliendo _____

15. quieran _____

14. yo sea _____

15. Ud. fuera _____

C.   Translate into English:

1. seríamos _____

2. fuimos _____

3. quisiste _____

4. habré sido _____

5. fueses _____

6. he sabido _____

7. habremos sabido _____

8. queramos _____

9. sabréis _____

10. erais _____

11. él supo _____

12. él había salido _____

13. ellos querían _____

14. sabríais _____

15. hayan salido _____

16. hubiéramos sabido _____

17. yo sea _____

18. él quisiera _____

19. salieran _____

20. supiéramos _____

Mastery Test

Write in Spanish:

1. he might know _____

2. you (pl., fam.) have gone out _____

_____

3. he would want _____

4. I was not (pret) _____

5. you (pl., fam.) have known _____

_____

6. we are _____

7. he may go out _____

8. you (s., fam.) will want _____

_____

9. we were knowing _____

10. he was (imperf.) _____

11. we were wanting _____

12. we might not go out _____

13. you (pl., fam.) will know _____

_____

14. they may be _____

15. I may have wanted _____

16. you (s., for.) will not be _____

_____

17. they will have known _____

18. they went out _____

19. you (s., fam.) had wanted _____

_____

20. we are not going out _____

21. I may have known _____

22. is he? _____

23. you (s., fam.) used to go out _____

_____

24. I did not want _____

25. they would have known _____

_____

26. don't they want? _____

27. we have been _____

_____

28. he will go out _____

29. we should know _____

30. you (pl., for.) might want _____

31. I am going out _____

32. you (s., for.) knew _____

33. I have wanted _____

34. we might have been _____

35. you (s., fam.) may want _____

_____

36. would they go out? _____

37. I know _____

38. he might be _____

39. they were (pret.) _____

40. we will have been _____

Tener   to have, hold, possess

Present Indicative: tengo, *tienes, tiene,* tenemos, tenéis, *tienen*   I have, etc.

Imperfect: tenía, etc.   I was having, etc.

Preterit: *tuve, tuviste, tuvo, tuvimos, tuvisteis, tuvieron*   I had, etc.

Future: *tendré, tendrás, tendrá, tendremos, tendréis, tendrán*   I will have, etc.

Conditional: *tendría,* etc.   I would have, etc.

Present Participle: teniendo   having

Past Participle: tenido   had

Present Subjunctive: *tenga, tengas, tenga, tengamos, tengáis, tengan*   I may have, etc.

Imperfect Subjunctive: *tuviera* (*tuviese*), etc.   I might have, etc.

Present Perfect Subjunctive: haya tenido, etc.   I may have had, etc.

Pluperfect Subjunctive: hubiera (hubiese) tenido, etc.   I might have had, etc.

Others:
contener   to contain
detener   to stop
mantener   to maintain
retener   to retain
sostener   to sustain

Traer   to bring

Present Indicative: *traigo*, traes, trae, etc.   I bring, etc.

Imperfect: traía, etc.   I was bringing, etc.

Preterit: *traje, trajiste, trajo, trajimos, trajisteis, trajeron*   I brought, etc.

Future: traeré, etc.   I will bring, etc.

Conditional: traería, etc.   I would bring, etc.

Present Participle: *trayendo*   bringing

Past Participle: traído   brought

Present Subjunctive: *traiga, traigas, traiga, traigamos, traigáis, traigan*   I may bring, etc.

Imperfect Subjunctive: *trajera* (*trajese*), etc.   I might bring, etc.

Present Perfect Subjunctive: haya traído, etc.   I may have brought, etc.

Pluperfect Subjunctive: hubiera (hubiese) traído, etc.   I might have brought, etc.

Others:
contraer   to contract

Valer   to be worth

Present Indicative: *valgo*, vales, vale, valemos, valéis, valen   I am worth, etc.

Imperfect: valía, etc.   I was worth, etc.

Preterit: valí, valiste, etc.   I was worth.

Future: *valdré, valdrás, valdrá, valdremos, valdréis, valdrán*   I will be worth

Conditional: *valdría*, etc.   I would be worth, etc.

Present Participle: valiendo   being worth

Past Participle: valido   valued

Present Subjunctive: *valga, valgas, valga, valgamos, valgáis, valgan*   I may be worth, etc.

Imperfect Subjunctive: valiera (valiese), etc.   I might be worth, etc.

Present Perfect Subjunctive: haya valido, etc.   I may have been worth, etc.

Pluperfect Subjunctive: hubiera (hubiese) valido, etc.   I might have been worth, etc.

Venir   to come

Present Indicative: *vengo, vienes, viene*, venimos, venís, *vienen*   I come, etc.

Imperfect: venía, etc.   I was coming, etc.

Preterit: *vine, viniste, vino, vinimos, vinisteis, vinieron*   I came, etc.

Future: *vendré, vendrás, vendrá, vendremos, vendréis, vendrán*   I will come, etc.
Conditional: *vendría*, etc.   I would come, etc.
Present Participle: viniendo   coming
Past Participle: venido   come
Present Subjunctive: *venga, vengas, venga, vengamos, vengáis, vengan*   I may come, etc.
Imperfect Subjunctive: *viniera (viniese)* etc.   I might come, etc.
Present Perfect Subjunctive: haya venido, etc.   I may have come, etc.
Pluperfect Subjunctive: hubiera (hubiese) venido, etc.   I might have come, etc.

Others:
convenir   to be suitable, agree

Para practicar

Change the infinitives to the tense and person indicated:

Present indicative   yo

contraer	convenir	detener	mantener	sostener
_____	_____	_____	_____	_____

Present indicative   Ud.

mantener	venir	valer	retener	traer
_____	_____	_____	_____	_____

Future   ellos

convenir	detener	mantener	valer	sostener
_____	_____	_____	_____	_____

Preterit   él

contener	traer	convenir	sostener	detener
_____	_____	_____	_____	_____

Present subjunctive   tú

venir	mantener	contraer	contener	valer
_____	_____	_____	_____	_____

Imperfect subjunctive   nosotros

contraer	venir	tener	sostener	mantener
_____	_____	_____	_____	_____

Aplicación

Write in English:

1. él habrá venido _____
2. hayas traído _____
3. ellas tuvieron _____
4. valgamos _____
5. ellos traerán _____
6. tuve _____
7. valdríamos _____
8. ellas habían venido _____
9. teníamos _____
10. traerías _____
11. has valido _____
12. vienes _____
13. valdrás _____
14. él viniera _____
15. traje _____

16. tendré _____
17. él valiera _____
18. ellos tuvieran _____
19. él ha traído _____
20. ellos vengan _____
21. ellos traían _____
22. Ud. tendría _____
23. valíamos _____
24. habremos venido _____
25. traigas _____
26. Uds. tienen _____
27. yo valdría _____
28. tuvieras _____
29. trajéramos _____
30. venías _____

Mastery Test

Write in Spanish

1. she has not come _____
2. he had had _____
3. you (s., fam.) might bring _____
4. he was worth (pret) _____
5. we might have had _____
6. they had brought _____

7. you (pl., fam.) came _____
8. he used to bring _____
9. he had _____
10. they are worth _____
11. they would not have _____
12. she brought _____

13. they were coming _____

14. do you (s., fam.) have? _____

15. they may bring _____

16. he may come _____

17. we are not bringing _____

18. we will have _____

19. you (s., fam.) will be worth _____

20. do you (pl., fam.) have? _____

21. you (s., fam.) may not bring _____

22. I am coming _____

23. you (pl., for.) may have _____

24. I am not worth _____

25. you (s., fam.) may have come _____

26. he would not bring _____

27. they had _____

28. they brought _____

29. will they come? _____

30. you (pl., fam.) might have _____

31. he might be worth _____

32. you (s., fam.) used to have _____

33. let us bring _____

34. he has had _____

35. you (s., fam.) have brought _____

36. didn't they have? _____

37. it would not be worth _____

38. you (pl., fam.) are bringing _____

39. we might come _____

40. he might bring _____

ver to see

Present Indicative: *veo*, ves, ve, vemos, *veis*, ven   I see, etc.
Imperfect: veía, veías, veía veíamos, veíais, veían   I was seeing, etc.
Preterit: vi, viste, vio, vimos, visteis, vieron   I saw, etc.
Future: veré, etc.   I will see, etc.
Conditional: vería, etc.   I would see, etc.
Present Participle: viendo   seeing
Past Participle: visto   seen
Present Subjunctive: vea, veas, vea, veamos, veáis, vean   I may see, etc.
Imperfect Subjunctive: viera (viese), etc.   I might see, etc.
Present Perfect Subjunctive: haya *visto*, etc.   I may have seen, etc.
Pluperfect Subjunctive: hubiera (hubiese) *visto*   I might have seen, etc.

Irregular Past Participles

Besides the irregular verbs whose past participles have been listed previously, several verbs, otherwise regular, have irregular past participles. Common ones are:

abrir	*abierto*	*morir*	*muerto*
cubrir	*cubierto*	*resolver*	*resuelto*
escribir	*escrito*	*volver*	*vuelto*

Others:

descubrir (*descubierto*) to discover   *revolver* (*revuelto*) to stir

describir (*descrito*) to describe   *devolver* (*devuelto*) to give back, return

Aplicación

Write in English:

1. yo vea _____

2. ellos hubieran descubierto _____ _____

3. viéramos _____

4. hayas visto _____

5. verías _____

6. vimos _____

7. hemos descrito _____

8. él vea _____

9. él habrá muerto _____

10. Uds. veían _____

11. verás _____

12. yo había resuelto _____

13. vemos _____

14. viste _____

15. ellos habrían vuelto _____

Mastery Test

Write in Spanish:

1. we do not see _____

2. they were seeing _____

3. you (pl., fam.) might see _____ _____

4. he had not written _____

5. you (s., fam.) may see _____ _____

6. she did not see _____

7. have they discovered? _____

_____

8. I might have seen _____

9. we would see _____

10. he has not covered _____

11. I was seeing _____

12. she will not see _____

13. he may have seen _____

14. they would have opened _____

15. don't you (pl., fam.) see? _____

_____

Repaso de verbos irregulares

A. Write in English:

1. él habrá venido _____

2. Uds. tuvieron _____

3. ellos irían _____

4. Ud. dirá _____

5. fuiste _____

6. él querría _____

7. vemos _____

8. fui _____

9. traje _____

10. él salía _____

11. habrás sabido _____

12. ellos estuvieran _____

13. habíamos podido _____

14. yo habría puesto _____

15. ellas den _____

16. yo ande _____

17. ellas cayeran _____

18. valgamos _____

19. él había cabido _____

20. oíste _____

21. él habrá satisfecho _____

22. él no haría _____

23. conducimos _____

24. Uds. asirían _____

25. traducías _____

26. haya habido _____

27. ella dice _____

28. vamos _____

29. habíamos sido _____

30. Uds. tendrán _____

31. ellos venían _____

32. ellas hayan visto _____

33. Uds. quisieron _____

34. él traía _____

35. ellos dieron _____

36. estés _____

37. Ud. salía _____

38. poníais _____

39. podemos _____

40. sabremos _____

41. habíamos oído _____

42. habrás valido _____

43. yo haya hecho _____

44. satisfarás _____

45. caeré _____

46. ella anduvo _____

47. él quepa _____

48. habrá _____

49. ellos tradujeron _____

50. yo conduzca _____

B.   Write in Spanish:

1. they may be (*ser*) _____

2. we will have come _____

3. you (s., fam.) were saying _____

_____

4. dos he go? _____

5. we might see _____

6. they might have _____

7. you (s., fam.) had wanted _____

_____

8. I should bring _____

9. I may know _____

10. we are (*estar*) _____

11. you (s., fam.) will have put _____

_____

12. I was able (imperf) _____

13. we have not given _____

14. he did not go out _____

15. you (pl., fam.) may have fallen _____

_____

16. we were hearing _____

17. he fell _____

18. we would be worth _____

19. he walked _____

20. I fitted _____

21. I will not do _____

22. they used to translate _____

_____

23. they would have seized _____

_____

24. he led _____

25. you (s., fam.) may deduce _____

_____

26. there would be _____

27. he will have said _____

28. I would go _____

29. they may have seen _____

30. they may have _____

31. he was coming _____

32. she was wanting _____

33. you (pl., fam.) have been (*ser*) _____

_____

34. let us not bring _____

35. he doesn't know _____

36. you (s., fam.) could (pret) _____

_____

37. we will be (*estar*) _____

38. give! (pl.) _____

39. I would go out _____

40. you (pl., fam.) will put _____

_____

41. I may hear _____

42. we will not walk _____

43. I will fit _____

44. you (s., for.) have been worth _____

_____

45. we might satisfy _____

46. we did not do _____

47. I am falling _____

48. we may seize _____

49. they might have been (*ser*) _____

_____

50. he might lead _____

Repaso general 2

A. Write in English:

1. pensamos _____

2. Ud. abrió _____

3. pierdan _____

4. ella contesta _____

5. entiendo _____

6. llegué _____

7. Ud. dirá _____

8. él se divirtió _____

9. yo duermo _____

10. trajimos _____

11. hice _____

12. ellos vendrán _____

13. sepas _____

14. yo pusiera _____

15. podamos _____

16. Ud. escoja _____

17. volviéramos _____

18. ellos saquen _____

19. ellos distinguen _____

20. yo buscara _____

21. leeré _____

22. Uds. conocerían _____

23. ellos tendrán _____

24. di _____

25. verás _____

26. él insinúa _____

27. yo empiece _____

28. enviamos _____

29. yo haya jugado _____

30. yo confíe _____

B.   Write in Spanish:

1. We were writing _____

2. he understands _____

3. they live _____

4. they were traveling _____

5. you (s., fam.) keep _____

6. you (pl., for.) were bringing _____

7. do we say? _____

8. he wants _____

9. he dressed himself _____

10. they did not see _____

11. we went out _____

12. he might put _____

13. they have not done _____

14. I don't know (saber) _____

15. you (s., fam.) could (pret.) _____
_____

16. we directed _____

17. I looked for _____

18. they might choose _____

19. explain! (pl., for.) _____

20. he may arrive _____

21. you (s., fam.) are worth _____

22. did they read? _____

23. you (s., fam.) might give _____
_____

24. let's not go _____

25. he may have _____

26. they may play _____

27. I denied _____

28. he may continue _____

29. I did not begin _____

30. they may send _____

Repaso general 3

A. Write in English:

1. empecé _____

2. yo juegue _____

3. negábamos _____

4. ella continúa _____

5. ellos enviarán _____

6. Ud. consigue _____

7. tuve _____

8. condujiste _____

9. yo salía _____

10. supieron _____

11. él oiría _____

12. Ud. cabe _____

13. él ponga _____

14. podríamos _____

15. vengo _____

16. ellos habrán muerto _____

17. yo reía _____

18. él contribuía _____

19. él destruye _____

20. Ud. poseía _____

21. construyan _____

22. él pierde _____

23. servíamos _____

24. él conocía _____

25. ella hirió _____

26. yo piense _____

27. echaron _____

28. él habrá perdido _____

29. escuchabas _____

30. ella había vuelto _____

B. Write in Spanish:

1. you (pl, fam.) were playing _____

_____

2. they might begin _____

3. I continue _____

4. I may trust _____

5. they do not read _____

6. he did not want _____

7. they would be (ser) _____

8. I am not correcting _____

9. I went _____

10. he said _____

11. I may see _____

12. you (s., for.) were falling _____

_____

13. I did _____

14. I have put _____

15. they will go out _____

16. I may read _____

17. we had slept _____

18. we might laugh _____

19. he may die _____

20. they did not believe _____

21. I sent _____

22. do you (pl., fam.) consent? _____

_____

23. they may destroy _____

24. he was repeating _____

25. we used to lose _____

26. you (s., fam.) do not return _____

_____

27. we were spending _____

28. I was living _____

29. you (pl., fam.) understood _____

_____

30. they have opened _____

Final Review

Featuring a mixture of reflexive, stem-changing, and irregular verbs, as well as verbs with orthographic changes, the verbs in this final review will reinforce your command of the kinds of conjugations you have learned throughout the book.

Moler   to grind

Present Indicative: *muelo, mueles, muele,* molemos, moléis, *muelen*   I grind, etc.

Imperfect: molía, etc.   I was grinding, etc.

Preterit: molí, etc.   I ground, etc.

Future: moleré, etc.   I will grind, etc.

Conditional: molería, etc.   I would grind, etc.

Present Participle: moliendo   grinding

Past Participle: molido   ground

Present Subjunctive: *muela, muelas, muela,* molamos, moláis, *muelan*   I may grind, etc.

Imperfect Subjunctive: moliera (moliese), etc.   I might grind, etc.

Present Perfect Subjunctive: haya molido, etc.   I may have ground, etc.

Pluperfect Subjunctive: hubiera (hubiese) molido, etc.   I might have ground, etc.

Fregar   to scrub

Present Indicative: *friego, friegas, friega,* fregamos, fregáis, *friegan*   I scrub, etc.

Imperfect: fregaba, etc.   I was scrubbing, etc.

Preterit: fregué, etc.   I scrubbed, etc.

Future: fregaré, etc.   I will scrub, etc.

Conditional: fregaría, etc.   I would scrub, etc.

Present Participle: fregando   scrubbing

Past Participle: fregado   scrubbed

Present Subjunctive: *friegue, friegues, friegue,* freguemos, freguéis, *frieguen*   I may scrub, etc.

Imperfect Subjunctive: fregara (fregase), etc.   I might scrub, etc.

Present Perfect Subjunctive: haya fregado, etc.   I may have scrubbed, etc.

Pluperfect Subjunctive: hubiera (hubiese) fregado, etc.   I might have scrubbed, etc.

Descender   to descend

Present Indicative: *desciendo, desciendes, desciende,* descendemos, descendéis, *descienden*   I descend, etc.

Imperfect: descendía, etc.   I was descending, etc.

Preterit: descendí, etc.   I descended, etc.

Future: descenderé, etc.   I will descend, etc.

Conditional: descendería, etc.   I would descend, etc.

Present Participle: descendiendo   descending

Past Participle: descendido   descended
Present Subjunctive: *descienda*, *desciendas*, *descienda*, descendamos, descendáis, *desciendan*
      I may descend, etc.
Imperfect Subjunctive: descendiera (descendiese), etc.   I might descend, etc.
Present Perfect Subjunctive: haya descendido, etc.   I may have descended, etc.
Pluperfect Subjunctive: hubiera (hubiese) descendido, etc.   I might have descended, etc.

Yacer to lie, to rest

Present Indicative: *yazgo*, yaces, yace, yacemos, yacéis, yacen   I lie, etc.
Imperfect: yacía, etc.   I was lying, etc.
Preterit: yací, etc.   I lay, etc.
Future: yaceré, etc.   I will lie, etc.
Conditional: yacería, etc.   I would lie, etc.
Present Participle: yaciendo   lying
Past Participle: yacido   lain
Present Subjunctive: *yazga*, *yazgas*, *yazga*, *yazgamos*, *yazgáis*, *yazgan*   I may lie, etc.
Imperfect Subjunctive: yaciera (yaciese), etc.   I might lie, etc.
Present Perfect Subjunctive: haya yacido, etc.   I may have lain, etc.
Pluperfect Subjunctive: hubiera (hubiese) yacido, etc.   I might have lain, etc.

Torcer to twist

Present Indicative: *tuerzo*, *tuerces*, *tuerce*, torcemos, torcéis, *tuercen*   I twist, etc.
Imperfect: torcía, etc.   I was twisting, etc.
Preterit: torcí, etc.   I twisted, etc.
Future: torceré, etc.   I will twist, etc.
Conditional: torcería, etc.   I would twist, etc.
Present Participle: torciendo   twisting
Past Participle: torcido   twisted
Present Subjunctive: *tuerza*, *tuerzas*, *tuerza*, torzamos, torzáis, *tuerzan*   I may twist, etc.
Imperfect Subjunctive: torciera (torciese), etc.   I might twist, etc.
Present Perfect Subjunctive: haya torcido, etc.   I may have twisted, etc.
Pluperfect Subjunctive: hubiera (hubiese) torcido, etc.   I might have twisted, etc.

Surgir to arise, to spring up

Present Indicative: *surjo*, surges, surge, surgimos, surgís, surgen   I arise, etc.
Imperfect: surgía, etc.   I was arising, etc.
Preterit: surgí, etc.   I arose, etc.
Future: surgiré, etc.   I will arise, etc.
Conditional: surgiría, etc.   I would arise, etc.
Present Participle: surgiendo   arising

Past Participle: surgido   arisen

Present Subjunctive: *surja, surjas, surja, surjamos, surjáis, surjan*   I may arise, etc.

Imperfect Subjunctive: surgiera (surgiese), etc.   I might arise, etc.

Present Perfect Subjunctive: haya surgido, etc.   I may have arisen, etc.

Pluperfect Subjunctive: hubiera (hubiese) surgido, etc.   I might have arisen, etc.

Mecer   to swing, to rock

Present Indicative: *mezo*, meces, mece, mecemos, mecéis, mecen   I swing, etc.

Imperfect: mecía, etc.   I was swinging, etc.

Preterit: mecí, etc.   I swung, etc.

Future: meceré, etc.   I will swing, etc.

Conditional: mecería, etc.   I would swing, etc.

Present Participle: meciendo   swinging

Past Participle: mecido   swung

Present Subjunctive: *meza, mezas, meza, mezamos, mezáis, mezan*   I may swing, etc.

Imperfect Subjunctive: meciera (meciese), etc.   I might swing, etc.

Present Perfect Subjunctive: haya mecido, etc.   I may have swung, etc.

Pluperfect Subjunctive: hubiera (hubiese) mecido, etc.   I might have swung, etc.

Reñir   to quarrel, to fight

Present Indicative: *riño, riñes, riñe*, reñimos, reñís, *riñen*   I quarrel, etc.

Imperfect: reñía, etc.   I was quarrelling, etc.

Preterit: reñí, etc.   I quarrelled, etc.

Future: reñiré, etc.   I will quarrel, etc.

Conditional: reñiría, etc.   I would quarrel, etc.

Present Participle: riñendo   quarrelling

Past Participle: reñido   quarrelled

Present Subjunctive: *riña, riñas, riña, riñamos, riñáis, riñan*   I may quarrel, etc.

Imperfect Subjunctive: *riñera* (*riñese*), etc.   I might quarrel, etc.

Present Perfect Subjunctive: haya reñido, etc.   I may have quarrelled, etc.

Pluperfect Subjunctive: hubiera (hubiese) reñido, etc.   I might have quarrelled, etc.

Avergonzar   to embarrass

Present Indicative: *avergüenzo, avergüenzas, avergüenza*, avergonzamos, avergonzáis, *avergüenzan*   I embarrass, etc.

Imperfect: avergonzaba, etc.   I was embarrassing, etc.

Preterit: avergoncé, etc.   I embarrassed, etc.

Future: avergonzaré, etc.   I will embarrass, etc.

Conditional: avergonzaría, etc.   I would embarrass, etc.

Present Participle: avergonzando   embarrassing

Past Participle: avergonzado   embarrassed

Present Subjunctive: *avergüence, avergüences, avergüence*, avergoncemos, avergoncéis, *avergüencen*   I may embarrass, etc.

Imperfect Subjunctive: avergonzara (avergonzase), etc.   I might embarrass, etc.

Present Perfect Subjunctive: haya avergonzado, etc.   I may have embarrassed, etc.

Pluperfect Subjunctive: hubiera (hubiese) avergonzado, etc.   I might have embarrassed, etc.

Influir   to influence

Present Indicative: *influyo, influyes, influye*, influimos, influís, *influyen*   I influence, etc.

Imperfect: influía, etc.   I was influencing, etc.

Preterit: influí, etc.   I influenced, etc.

Future: influiré, etc.   I will influence, etc.

Conditional: influiría, etc.   I would influence, etc.

Present Participle: *influyendo*   influencing

Past Participle: influido   influenced

Present Subjunctive: *influya, influyas, influya, influyamos, influyáis, influyan*   I may influence, etc.

Imperfect Subjunctive: *influyera* (*influyese*), etc.   I might influence, etc.

Present Perfect Subjunctive: haya influido, etc.   I may have influenced, etc.

Pluperfect Subjunctive: hubiera (hubiese) influido, etc.   I might have influenced, etc.

Roer   to gnaw

Present Indicative: roo, roes, roe, roemos, roéis, roen   I gnaw, etc.

Imperfect: roía, etc.   I was gnawing, etc.

Preterit: roí, etc.   I gnawed, etc.

Future: roeré, etc.   I will gnaw, etc.

Conditional: roería, etc.   I would gnaw, etc.

Present Participle: *royendo*   gnawing

Past Participle: roído   gnawed

Present Subjunctive: roa, roas, roa, roamos, roáis, roan   I may gnaw

Imperfect Subjunctive: *royera* (*royese*), etc.   I might gnaw, etc.

Present Perfect Subjunctive: haya roído, etc.   I may have gnawed, etc.

Pluperfect Subjunctive: hubiera (hubiese) roído, etc.   I might have gnawed, etc.

Erguir(se)   to straighten (oneself) up

Present Indicative: (me) *yergo*, (te) *yergues*,(se) *yergue*, (nos) erguimos, (os) erguís, (se) *yerguen*   I straighten (myself) up, etc

Imperfect: erguía, etc.   I was straightening up, etc.

Preterit: erguí, etc.   I straightened up, etc.

Future: erguiré, etc.   I will straighten up, etc.

Conditional: erguiría, etc.   I would straighten up, etc.

Present Participle: *irguiendo*   straightening up

Past Participle: erguido   straightened up

Present Subjunctive: *yerga, yergas, yerga, yergamos, irgáis, yergan*   I may straighten up

Imperfect Subjunctive: *irguiera* (*irguiese*), etc.   I might straighten up, etc.

Present Perfect Subjunctive: haya erguido, etc.   I may have straightened up, etc.

Pluperfect Subjunctive: hubiera (hubiese) erguido, etc.   I might have straightened up, etc.

Discernir   to discern

Present Indicative: *discierno, disciernes, discierne*, discernimos, discernís, *disciernen*   I discern, etc.

Imperfect: discernía, etc.   I was discerning, etc.

Preterit: discerní, etc.   I discerned, etc.

Future: discerniré, etc.   I will discern, etc.

Conditional: discerniría, etc.   I would discern, etc.

Present Participle: discerniendo   discerning

Past Participle: discernido   discerned

Present Subjunctive: *discierna, disciernas, discierna*, discernamos, discernáis, disciernan   I may discern

Imperfect Subjunctive: discerniera (discerniese), etc.   I might discern, etc.

Present Perfect Subjunctive: haya discernido, etc.   I may have discerned, etc.

Pluperfect Subjunctive: hubiera (hubiese) discernido, etc.   I might have discerned, etc.

Zurcir   to mend, to darn

Present Indicative: *zurzo*, zurces, zurce, zurcimos, zurcís, zurcen   I mend, etc.

Imperfect: zurcía, etc.   I was mending, etc.

Preterit: zurcí, etc.   I mended, etc.

Future: zurciré, etc.   I will mend, etc.

Conditional: zurciría, etc.   I would mend, etc.

Present Participle: zurciendo   mending

Past Participle: zurcido   mended

Present Subjunctive: *zurza, zurzas, zurza, zurzamos, zurzáis, zurzan*   I may mend

Imperfect Subjunctive: zurciera (zurciese), etc.   I might mend, etc.

Present Perfect Subjunctive: haya zurcido, etc.   I may have mended, etc.

Pluperfect Subjunctive: hubiera (hubiese) zurcido, etc.   I might have mended, etc.

Entrenar(se) to train (oneself)

Present Indicative: (me) entreno, (te) entrenas, (se) entrena, (nos) entrenamos, (os) entrenáis, (se) entrenan I train, etc.

Imperfect: entrenaba, etc. I was training, etc.

Preterit: entrené, etc. I trained, etc.

Future: entrenaré, etc. I will train, etc.

Conditional: entrenaría, etc. I would train, etc.

Present Participle: entrenando   training

Past Participle: entrenado trained

Present Subjunctive: (me) entrene, (te) entrenes, (se) entrene, (nos) entrenemos, (os) entrenéis, (se) entrenen I may train

Imperfect Subjunctive: entrenara (entrenase), etc. I might train, etc.

Present Perfect Subjunctive: haya entrenado, etc. I may have trained, etc.

Pluperfect Subjunctive: hubiera (hubiese) entrenado, etc. I might have trained, etc.

Enojar(se) to get angry (oneself)

Present Indicative: (me) enojo, (te) enojas, (se) enoja, (nos) enojamos, (os) enojáis, (se) enojan I get angry, etc.

Imperfect: enojaba, etc. I was getting angry, etc.

Preterit: enojé, etc. I got angry, etc.

Future: enojaré, etc. I will get angry, etc.

Conditional: enojaría, etc. I would get angry, etc.

Present Participle: enojando getting angry

Past Participle: enojado gotten angry

Present Subjunctive: (me) enoje, (te) enojes, (se) enoje, (nos) enojemos, (os) enojéis, (se) enojen I may get angry

Imperfect Subjunctive: enojara (enojase), etc. I might get angry, etc.

Present Perfect Subjunctive: haya enojado, etc. I may have gotten angry, etc.

Pluperfect Subjunctive: hubiera (hubiese) enojado, etc. I might have gotten angry, etc.

Para practicar 1

Write the infinitives in the present, imperfect, and preterit tenses in the person indicated:

1. yo (aprender) _____

2. Ud. (zurcir) _____

3. ella (pecar) _____

4. nosotros (avergonzar) _____

5. vosotros (erguirse) _____

6. tú (sollozar) _____

7. ellas (vestirse) _____

8. ellos (caber) _____

9. Ud. (oler) _____

10. yo (yacer) _____

11. él (exponer) _____

12. Uds. (apaciguar) _____

13. tú (graduarse) _____

14. yo (roer) _____

15. ella (enojarse) _____

16. nosotros (poseer) _____

17. tú (almorzar) _____

18. ellos (revolver) _____

19. Ud. (huir) _____

20. yo (salir) _____

21. ellas (desnegar) _____

22. vosotros (suponer) _____

23. él (levantarse) _____

24. nosotros (compadecer) _____

25. tú (ahogar) _____

Para practicar 2

A.   Change to the plural of the same tense:

1. voy _____

2. has estado _____

3. él arriesgaría _____

4. ella había querido _____

5. se divirtió _____

6. te levantaste _____

7. hubiera escuchado _____

8. estoy traduciendo _____

9. yo haya fregado _____

10. dormirías _____

B.   Change to the singular person of the corresponding compound tense:

1. avergonzáramos _____

2. tomabais _____

3. hablaríamos _____

4. dormirán _____

5. no desconfíen _____

6. estamos comiendo _____

7. dijimos _____

8. sintiesen _____

9. oleremos _____

10. vistieseis _____

Para practicar 3

A. Write the present perfect in the person indicated:

1. yo (estudiar) _____

2. María (necesitar) _____

3. nosotros (contar) _____

4. vosotros (ofender) _____

5. ustedes (decir) _____

6. tú (ser) _____

7. yo (moler) _____

8. Ernesto (suponer) _____

9. Luis y María (dormir) _____

10. vosotros (describir) _____

B. Write the conditional in the person indicated:

1. Juan complace _____

2. vosotros ofenderéis _____

3. tú has dicho _____

4. ellas sostendrán _____

5. Ud. se habrá entrenado _____

6. nosotros nos hubiésemos mecido _____

_____

7. yo extinga _____

8. María y Ana habían sabido _____

9. Uds. venderán _____

10. ¿acertará él? _____

Para practicar 4

A. Write the present participles of the following infinitives:

1. escuchar _____

2. carecer _____

3. medir _____

4. estar _____

5. ser _____

6. perseguir _____

7. advertir _____

8. vestirse _____

9. servir _____

10. huir _____

B. Write the past participles of the following infinitives:

1. abrir _____
2. ejercer _____
3. suponer _____
4. revolver _____
5. hacer _____

6. descubrir _____
7. agradecer _____
8. satisfacer _____
9. costar _____
10. volver _____

Para practicar 5

A. Write the infinitives in the present indicative in the person indicated:

Ud.

servir	influir	vivir	decaer	oler
_____	_____	_____	_____	_____

B. Write the infinitives in the preterit in the person indicated:

yo

reñir	sonreír	seguir	contraer	resolver
_____	_____	_____	_____	_____

C. Write the infinitives in the present subjunctive in the person indicated:

vosotros

comprender	convenir	encontrar	insinuar	repetir
_____	_____	_____	_____	_____

D. Write the infinitives in the future perfect in the person indicated:

ella

morir	perder	escribir	proponer	caber
_____	_____	_____	_____	_____

E.   Write the infinitives in the imperfect indicative in the person indicated:

nosotros

oír   enriquecerse   desconocer   negar   unir

_____   _____   _____   _____   _____

Para practicar 6

Write the infinitives in the present subjunctive in the person indicated:

tú

rascar   asir   fregar   torcer   cargar

_____   _____   _____   _____   _____

nosotros

escuchar   conducir   descontinuar   destruir   negar

_____   _____   _____   _____   _____

él

contraer   creer   delinquir   valer   contestar

_____   _____   _____   _____   _____

vosotros

secar   gemir   habituarse   aborrecer   esconder

_____   _____   _____   _____   _____

yo

dormir   surgir   impedir   preparar   decir

_____   _____   _____   _____   _____

Aplicación 1

Write in English:

1. yo tenga _____

2. Juan y Pedro se diviertan _____

3. habías salido _____

4. ellas estaban consintiendo _____

_____

5. habré escrito _____

6. él hablaría _____

7. Uds. habían revuelto _____

8. ellos midieron _____

9. yo advertía _____

10. Ud. sintiera _____

11. hubieseis movido _____

12. ¿cuándo empezarás? _____

13. ¡ven! _____

14. te hubieras divertido _____

15. ella habría creído _____

16. ¡no confiéis! _____

17. ¿vas a jugar? _____

18. secaremos _____

19. yo estaba limpiando _____

20. ella necesitó _____

21. podríamos _____

22. ofendiste _____

23. Ud. encuentre _____

24. Juan reía _____

25. tuvisteis _____

26. nos vestíamos _____

27. habremos sollozado _____

28. él tuvo _____

29. estábamos estudiando _____

30. no habíamos encontrado _____

31. durmiéramos _____

32. hayas viajado _____

33. Uds. conocerían _____

34. ellos necesitan _____

35. yo midiera _____

Aplicación 2

Change each verb to express past time in the same person and mood:

1. dormimos _____
2. influyas _____
3. él abre _____
4. he revuelto _____
5. habéis elegido _____
6. Uds. ruegan _____
7. desconocéis _____
8. no beban _____
9. somos _____
10. pasaremos _____
11. encontramos _____
12. exponga _____
13. se enriquezcan _____

14. creemos _____
15. habéis aceptado _____
16. carguen _____
17. son _____
18. distinguís _____
19. hemos convocado _____
20. compitas _____
21. están corrigiendo _____
22. obedezcamos _____
23. finjáis _____
24. están _____
25. aborrezceremos _____

Aplicación 3

Change from singular to plural in the same tense:

1. estoy oliendo _____
2. viví _____
3. yo admiraba _____
4. él merecía _____
5. hayas desaparecido _____
6. Ud. habría ejercido _____
7. obligues _____

8. gemirás _____
9. ella compusiera _____
10. yo aprendería _____
11. ella riñó _____
12. él haya conseguido _____
13. ¡corra! _____
14. yo habría pensado _____

15. huyas _____

16. me estoy habituando a _____

_____

17. ha _____

18. has colgado _____

19. hubieras desconfiado _____

20. no esparzas _____

21. pecaré _____

22. sonreíste _____

23. Ud. haya dormido _____

24. me sentaría _____

25. habías erguido _____

Aplicación 4

Change each simple tense to a corresponding compound tense, keeping the person of the original verb:

1. hable _____

2. comieron _____

3. estuvisteis _____

4. pasarán _____

5. no confiarais _____

6. extingas _____

7. moveremos _____

8. muelan _____

9. sintáis _____

10. persigamos _____

11. entrarás _____

12. carecieses _____

13. te enriquecerás _____

14. ofrecen _____

15. decaerías _____

16. será _____

17. colocaríais _____

18. huyó _____

19. influyo _____

20. acordaran _____

21. aprobaste _____

22. asistirías _____

23. llegaréis _____

24. delinquieseis _____

25. rió _____

140

Aplicación 5

Change from present to imperfect subjunctive:

1. necesitemos _____
2. ruegue _____
3. pagues _____
4. preparéis _____
5. ponga _____
6. produzca _____
7. Pedro y Elena abran _____ _____
8. apacigüe _____
9. impidan _____
10. mezan _____
11. compadezcáis _____
12. prosigas _____
13. paguen _____
14. complazca _____
15. juguemos _____
16. tenga _____
17. coloque _____
18. apagues _____
19. emprendamos _____
20. tome _____
21. repitáis _____
22. arriesguen _____
23. enseñe _____
24. satisfaga _____
25. encoja _____

Mastery Test 1

Translate into Spanish:

1. I will decide _____
2. we are demanding _____
3. they might have seized _____
4. Juan and Pedro ate _____
5. you (pl., fam.) would spend _____
6. I have lied _____
7. she listens _____

8. we were coming _____

9. you (pl., for.) might read _____

10. he has remembered _____

11. I shall not fall _____

12. we had _____

13. I might have paid _____

14. we may reach _____

15. I return _____

16. he has _____

17. he would not have prayed _____

18. she may have seen _____

19. we were quarreling _____

20. you (s., fam.) used to sleep _____

21. he walked _____

22. did she scatter? _____

23. you (pl., fam.) replied _____

24. were you (s., for.) serving? _____

25. will she run? _____

26. we smile _____

27. Gil, Ana and Luis may seize _____

28. they used to carry _____

29. I do not believe it _____

30. I will have ground _____

31. they may not convince _____

32. it is raining _____

33. they sold _____

34. you (sin., for.) returned _____

35. they would have dressed _____

Mastery Test 2

Translate into English:

1. comeré _____

2. hubierais jugado _____

3. yazgo _____

4. competíamos _____

5. él vencería _____

6. Ud. cabe _____

7. ella había convencido _____

8. ellas tropezaron _____

9. Uds. estaban preparando _____

10. ellos nieguen _____

11. admiro _____

12. he comido _____

13. ellas hablarán _____

14. ¡no decidas! _____

15. Uds. hubiesen hablado _____

16. yo mantenga _____

17. hemos dicho _____

18. Ud. habría encontrado _____

19. me lavaba _____

20. estabais pensando _____

21. ellos no cargaban _____

22. habías avergonzado _____

23. desafiaremos _____

24. habré encendido _____

25. exigís _____

26. ella había supuesto _____

27. Uds. están mintiendo _____

28. María y José pagarán _____

_____

29. ejercisteis _____

30. se vistieron _____

31. estábamos mordiendo _____

32. yo continuaría _____

33. Ud. indicara _____

34. sabías _____

35. ¡no pares! _____

Mastery Test 3

Translate into Spanish using reflexive verbs:

1. he may have washed _____

2. I dressed _____

3. we have amused ourselves _____

4. she combed her hair _____

5. they used to wash _____

6. you (pl., for.) have gotten up _____

7. they might remember _____

8. he was washing _____

9. I shall grow accustomed to _____

10. you (pl., fam.) washed _____

11. she might have gotten angry _____

12. let's dress! _____

13. I am going to bed _____

14. they may wash _____

15. you (sin., fam.) would have remembered _____

16. she is training _____

17. he had gone to bed _____

18. they will have tried hard _____

19. we may sit _____

20. she is becoming rich _____

21. Miguel has gotten up _____

22. I might straighten up _____

23. they grew accustomed to _____

24. she used to amuse herself _____

25. I shall get up _____

26. do not sit! (pl., fam.) _____

27. they are dressing _____

28. we might graduate _____

29. are we trying hard? _____

30. you (sin., for.) may have washed _____

31. they would go to bed _____

32. I amuse myself _____

33. María used to comb her hair _____

34. he would have trained _____

35. we got angry _____

Mastery Test 4

Change each simple tense into a compound one in the same person:

1. tome _____

2. medimos _____

3. desconfiarás _____

4. obedece _____

5. se acostaba _____

6. ejercieron _____

7. distinguiese _____

8. dispongas _____

9. influyáis _____

10. sollozaréis _____

11. acierte _____

12. expusiéramos _____

13. elegirán _____

14. hablaríamos _____

15. me acuesto _____

16. subes _____

17. aborrecerán _____

18. moveríamos _____

19. quepamos _____

20. obedecéis _____

21. oliesen _____

22. eligió _____

23. corrigiéramos _____

24. explicase _____

25. llueve _____

Repaso 1

Write in English:

1. él habrá venido _____

2. olisteis _____

3. digas _____

4. Elena rió _____

5. somos _____

6. riño _____

7. Ud. cupo _____

8. delinquiéramos _____

9. Uds. quieran _____

10. estamos cayendo _____

11. ellos anduvieron _____

12. él huele _____

13. hemos conducido _____

14. habrías dicho _____

15. ella erraba _____

16. dierais _____

17. dedujiste _____

18. yo haya dicho _____

19. ellas bendijeran _____

20. yo iría _____

21. habrás hecho _____

22. ellos satisfarán _____

23. vayamos _____

24. no pondrías _____

25. Ud. saliese _____

Repaso 2

Change each verb to represent more than one person in the same tense:

1. acabo _____

2. hablas _____

3. comiste _____

4. habría partido _____

5. estudiará _____

6. ella comprenda _____

7. he preguntado _____

8. beberás _____

9. ella escuchaba _____

10. abrí _____

11. entraste _____

12. vivió _____

13. hubiera tomado _____

14. yo tema _____

15. habré estudiado _____

16. ¿se habrá graduado? _____

17. yo estaba llevando _____

18. él escribiría _____

19. comprenderé _____

20. Ud. entre _____

21. él haya leído _____

22. yo había vendido _____

23. has trabajado _____

24. ella prepararía _____

25. me hubiese amado _____

Repaso 3

Write in Spanish:

1. I may understand _____

2. you (s., fam.) might speak _____

3. we might have said _____

4. you (pl., for.) may not smile! _____

5. she might have disappeared _____

6. I may not discover _____

7. he may have slept _____

8. you (pl., fam.) might notice _____

9. we may lie _____

10. she might comb her hair _____

11. you (s., for.) may have mistrusted _____

12. they may learn _____

13. you (pl., fam.) might have stumbled _____

14. I might go _____

15. she may sell _____

16. Ana and Juan might compete _____

17. he may dress _____

18. we might have needed _____

19. they might have gone to bed _____

20. you (pl., for.) may have not twisted _____

21. she may remember _____

22. I would warm _____

23. we may have taught _____

24. he might follow _____

25. you (pl., fam.) may have arisen _____

Repaso 4

Write in English:

1. ella prepara _____

2. ¿están ellos entrando? _____

3. habremos impedido _____

4. llegué _____

5. habréis satisfecho _____

6. ellos están desconfiando _____

7. habíamos compuesto _____

8. ellos advertirían _____

9. él continuaba _____

10. yo me yergo _____

11. ¡bendícenos! _____

12. habrás analizado _____

13. detuviéramos _____

14. él conduzca _____

15. sollozarás _____

16. yo habría reñido _____

17. Elisa y Marta habían pensado _____

_____

18. consiguiésemos _____

19. estudiaríais _____

20. habremos valido _____

21. ellos viviesen _____

22. ¡no mintáis! _____

23. ella haya impuesto _____

24. Uds. hubieran perseguido _____

25. estabas mostrando _____

26. ellos se acostaran _____

27. ella zurció _____

28. Ud. había abrazado _____

29. ella querría _____

30. nevará _____

31. Uds. hayan descendido _____

32. vivamos _____

33. él no coloque _____

34. erais _____

35. yo haya roído _____

36. Ud. habría hecho _____

37. compongo _____

38. fuésemos (to go) _____

39. hubiérais partido _____

40. ellas consiguiesen _____

Repaso 5

Write in Spanish:

1. I will go _____

2. it's raining _____

3. you (s., for.) may sleep _____

4. we had thrown _____

5. they were playing _____

6. she has marked _____

7. Juan and Ana might know _____

_____

8. she will have exercised _____

9. I would conduct _____

10. enter! (s., fam.) _____

11. we may have disposed _____

12. she does not deserve _____

13. you (pl., for.) might have found _____

14. let's not go _____

15. they may stop _____

16. he does listen _____

17. we might wash _____

18. I would bother _____

19. María will break the law _____

20. she is worth _____

21. we are travelling _____

22. I am combing my hair _____

23. you (pl., fam.) may influence _____

_____

24. he had conquered _____

25. they would explain _____

Repaso 6

A. Change each verb from singular to plural in the same tense:

1. parto _____

2. comías _____

3. él unía _____

4. ella había salido _____

5. ¡acuéstese! _____

6. ¡no me pidas! _____

7. yo corregiría _____

8. Ud. haya confesado _____

9. ella se habrá acostado _____

10. discernió _____

11. yo me hubiese despertado _____

_____

12. desaparecerás _____

13. bendices _____

14. yo huela _____

15. se peinó _____

B. Write the following infinitives in the present subjunctive in the person indicated:

1. tú (marcar) _____

2. ustedes (repetir) _____

3. nosotros (salir) _____

4. yo (caber) _____

5. él (consentir) _____

6. vosotros (explicar) _____

7. Ana y Juan (aborrecer) _____

8. yo (elegir) _____

9. ellos (haber) _____

10. ustedes (hacer) _____

11. ellas (ir) _____

12. nosotros (erguir) _____

13. tú (encoger) _____

14. usted (encontrar) _____

15. ella (complacer) _____

Repaso 7

A. Write the present indicative of the following infinitives in the person indicated:

ella

errar	huir	cerrar	gemir	morir	negar
_____	_____	_____	_____	_____	_____

disponer	encontrar	proseguir	haber
_____	_____	_____	_____

B. Write the present subjunctive of the following infinitives in the person indicated:

nosotros

contar	revolver	castigar	surgir	lavar(se)	conducir
_____	_____	_____	_____	_____	_____

parecer	sacar	esconder	santiguar
_____	_____	_____	_____

C. Write the imperfect subjunctive of the following infinitives in the person indicated:

yo

colegir	mantener	cubrir	perseguir	decaer	andar
_____	_____	_____	_____	_____	_____

acoger	querer	dormir	influir
_____	_____	_____	_____

Repaso 8

Change each simple tense into the corresponding compound tense in the same person:

1. acertaba _____
2. hablen _____
3. hablarían _____
4. dijimos _____

5. mantenemos _____
6. hacíais _____
7. corrían _____
8. advirtieras _____

9. descubriré ————————————

10. colocaban ————————————

11. almuercen ————————————

12. se dispusiese ————————————

13. adornáis ————————————

14. me vestiré ————————————

15. royéramos ————————————

16. abrías ————————————

17. ofrezco ————————————

18. hirieran ————————————

19. fatigüéis ————————————

20. supo ————————————

Answer Key

PRESENT

Para practicar

pp. 2–5

(1)	(2)	(1)	(2)	(1)	(2)
acabo	tomo	vendo	bebo	vivo	recibo
acabas	tomas	vendes	bebes	vives	recibes
acaba	toma	vende	bebe	vive	recibe
acaba	toma	vende	bebe	vive	recibe
acabamos	tomamos	vendemos	bebemos	vivimos	recibimos
acabáis	tomáis	vendéis	bebéis	vivís	recibís
acaban	toman	venden	beben	viven	reciben
acaban	toman	venden	beben	viven	reciben

estudio, comprendo, temo, necesito, parto, enseño, vendo.

hablas, asistes, abres, bebes, preguntas, tomas, escuchas.

contesta, abre, aprende, entra, lee, vive, come.

escribe, estudia, acaba, teme, parte, comprende, vende.

aprendemos, asistimos, tomamos, escuchamos, hablamos, vivimos, tememos.

habláis, asistís, bebéis, leéis, tomáis, lleváis, enseñáis.

comen, escriben, necesitan, entran, acaban, leen, viven.

temen, llevan, estudian, preguntan, contestan, comprenden, parten.

Aplicación

pp. 5–6

A.
1. tomamos
2. aprende
3. venden
4. asisto
5. contestas
6. bebe
7. abrimos
8. necesita
9. tomáis
10. lee
11. aprendo
12. tememos
13. recibís
14. escriben
15. abre
16. enseñamos
17. contesto
18. estudiamos
19. abro
20. toma
21. pregunta
22. leen
23. reciben
24. temes
25. leemos

Aplicación (*cont.*)

B.
1. escribimos,
   we write
2. ellos contestan,
   they answer
3. vivimos,
   we live
4. Uds. necesitan,
   you need
5. ellos beben,
   they drink
6. aprendéis,
   you learn
7. ellos venden,
   they sell
8. asistimos,
   we attend
9. Uds. enseñan,
   you teach
10. abrís,
    you open
11. Uds. comprenden,
    you understand
12. ellas escuchan,
    they listen
13. teméis,
    you fear
14. ellas preguntan,
    they ask
15. Uds. leen,
    you read
16. tomamos,
    we take
17. recibimos,
    we receive
18. ellos estudian,
    they study
19. necesitamos,
    we need
20. escribís,
    you write

Mastery Test

pp. 6—7

1. contestamos
2. vendéis
3. él pregunta
4. ellos venden
5. no necesitamos
6. estudiamos
7. aprendo
8. ¿escuchan ellos?
9. él no lee
10. Ud. no entra
11. trabajamos
12. ¿escribes?
13. ellos preguntan
14. Uds. toman
15. vendo
16. ella no trabaja
17. ellos no creen
18. ellos esconden
19. él escribe
20. ¿temes?
21. vivimos
22. él enseña
23. ella teme
24. recibís
25. él abre
26. ellos no toman
27. asistimos
28. ¿vende él?
29. estudio
30. creo
31. ellos unen
32. ellos no abren
33. enseñas
34. él asiste
35. preguntamos
36. ¿aprenden Uds?
37. ella bebe
38. ¿estudias?
39. Ud. vive
40. ellos entran

IMPERFECT

Para practicar

pp. 8—10

tomaba, metía, vivía, compraba, sentía, viajaba, corría.

aprendías, subías, pasabas, guardabas, cosías, esperabas, acababas.

tocaba, amaba, sabía, jugaba, viajaba, comprendía, escribía.

echaba, preparaba, leía, vivía, abría, corría, trabajaba.

estudiábamos, vendíamos, subíamos, comprendíamos, abríamos, preparábamos, tomábamos.

escribíais, trabajabais, comíais, bebíais, recibíais, comprabais, llevabais.

pasaban, caminaban, respondían, subían, hablaban, abrían, sacaban.

acababan, salían, contestaban, vivían, guardaban, corrían, viajaban.

Aplicación

pp. 10–11

A.
1. hablaba
2. vivíamos
3. sabía
4. conocían
5. pedían
6. corríamos
7. partías
8. pasaba
9. esperabais
10. acababan
11. caminaba
12. comprendía
13. tomaban
14. escribía
15. amaba
16. conocíais
17. bebías
18. comprábamos
19. subían
20. corría
21. respondía
22. guardabas
23. aprendía
24. llevaban
25. pasabais

B.
1. contestábamos, we were answering
2. vendías, you were selling
3. preguntaba, he was asking
4. aprendía, I was learning
5. escuchaban, they were listening
6. Ud. escribía, you were writing
7. aprendían, they were learning
8. Ud. estudiaba, you were studying
9. vivíamos, we were living
10. temía, he was fearing
11. abría, he was opening
12. enseñaban, they were teaching
13. asistía, he was attending
14. tomábamos, we were taking
15. leía, I was reading
16. Uds. bebían, you were drinking
17. temía, I was fearing
18. recibían, they were receiving
19. necesitaba, I was needing
20. Uds. vivían, you were living
21. abríamos, we were opening
22. contestabais, you were answering
23. tomabas, you were taking
24. bebía, he was drinking
25. abrías, you were opening

Mastery Test

pp. 11–12

1. vivían
2. trabajábamos
3. no vendías
4. vivíamos
5. no necesitaban
6. Ud. aprendía
7. creía
8. preguntabais
9. temía
10. ¿comprendías?
11. enseñaba
12. Uds. tomaban
13. no escuchábamos
14. vendía
15. Uds. abrían
16. ¿recibían?
17. asistíamos
18. estudiabas
19. leía
20. vivían
21. Uds. no escondían
22. recibía
23. no comprendían
24. comía
25. Ud. vendía
26. no tomabas
27. escuchaban
28. ¿asistía?
29. necesitabais
30. contestaba

PRETERIT

Para practicar

pp. 13—15

viajé, trabajé, estudié, comí, vendí, insistí, recibí.

uniste, acabaste, compraste, rompiste, corriste, abriste, tomaste.

comió, asistió, echó, preparó, subió, pasó, trabajó.

viajó, habló, aprendió, resistió, llamó, respondió, echó.

trabajamos, compramos, amamos, vendimos, bebimos, corrimos, vivimos.

estudiasteis, comisteis, abristeis, tomasteis, viajasteis, subisteis, pasasteis.

trabajaron, compraron, hablaron, aprendieron, temieron, escribieron, viajaron.

guardaron, comprendieron, asistieron, abrieron, pasaron, echaron, bebieron.

Aplicación

pp. 15—16

A.
1. llevé
2. abrimos
3. llegaste
4. comieron
5. bebió
6. metisteis
7. viajaron
8. vivió
9. pasaron
10. vendieron
11. abrí
12. asistió
13. recibieron
14. tomamos
15. temisteis
16. abrió
17. escribieron
18. necesitaron
19. vendiste
20. bebimos
21. aprendieron
22. tomé
23. estudió
24. bebió
25. recibí

B.
1. tomamos, tomábamos
2. enseñaron, enseñaban
3. contestó, contestaba
4. recibieron, recibían
5. aprendió, aprendía
6. asistí, asistía
7. temimos, temíamos
8. vendieron, vendían
9. aprendí, aprendía
10. contesté, contestaba
11. tomaron, tomaban
12. abrió, abría
13. necesitó, necesitaba
14. recibiste, recibías
15. trabajó, trabajaba
16. echaron, echaban
17. subieron, subían
18. comprendí, comprendía
19. corrió, corría
20. trabajé, trabajaba
21. preparó, preparaba
22. guardaron, guardaban
23. pasamos, pasábamos
24. viajé, viajaba
25. echaste, echabas

Mastery Test

pp. 16–17

1. contestamos
2. vendieron
3. aprendí
4. ¿escuchaste?
5. no preguntó
6. Ud. escondió
7. tomamos
8. no bebieron
9. asistimos
10. enseñé
11. preguntaste
12. trabajaron
13. Uds. unieron
14. viví
15. contestasteis
16. Uds. escribieron
17. comprendió
18. no aprendieron
19. escribimos
20. ¿estudió?
21. vendiste
22. enseñó
23. asistió
24. vendí
25. vivisteis
26. recibieron
27. asistí
28. preguntaron
29. bebimos
30. Ud. estudió
31. no contesté
32. ¿abrieron Uds.?
33. no comprendieron
34. no necesitaste
35. vendimos
36. ¿tomó Ud.?
37. no recibimos
38. temió
39. escribí
40. ¿preguntasteis?

Repaso (Present, imperfect, preterit)

pp. 18–19

1. vivían
2. abría
3. no trabajaron
4. subíamos
5. comprendo
6. no tomaron
7. corría
8. contestaron
9. trabajo
10. preparaste
11. Uds. estudiaban
12. guardan
13. pasábamos
14. viajé
15. Ud. necesita
16. no vivía
17. Uds. abrían
18. escribía
19. subo
20. comprendió
21. escribía
22. respondes
23. comprendimos
24. no aprendisteis
25. preparan
26. aprendemos
27. corrimos
28. Uds. pasaban
29. trabajaron
30. asistimos
31. no escribíamos
32. eché
33. estudiábamos
34. trabajé
35. vivíamos
36. guardamos
37. comprendiste
38. asistieron
39. vendíamos
40. paso
41. viví
42. temes
43. escuchó
44. no guardasteis
45. bebe
46. guardaban
47. partió
48. Ud. temió
49. subimos
50. no contesto

FUTURE

Para practicar

pp. 20−22

compraré, hablaré, leeré, viviré, sentiré, seré, asistiré.

estudiarás, encontrarás, correrás, tomarás, venderás, conocerás, partirás.

enseñará, perderá, dormirá, aprenderá, recibirá, abrirá, necesitará.

dudará, creerá, amará, escribirá, guardará, correrá, subirá.

contestaremos, temeremos, preguntaremos, subiremos, viajaremos, aprenderemos, viviremos.

prepararéis, echaréis, contestaréis, trabajaréis, viajaréis, responderéis, amaréis.

comprarán, leerán, sentirán, recibirán, decidirán, andarán, pasarán.

prepararán, aprenderán, echarán, viajarán, contestarán, correrán, marcharán.

Aplicación

pp. 22−23

A.
1. hablará
2. estaremos
3. será
4. encontrarán
5. leerá
6. dudaré
7. perderemos
8. enseñarás
9. dormiréis
10. andará
11. decidirás
12. compraré
13. vivirá
14. sentirá
15. beberá
16. estudiaréis
17. abrirá
18. venderás
19. escucharán
20. aprenderán
21. necesitará
22. contestará
23. temeremos
24. tomaré
25. recibirás

B.
1. vivirán
   they will live
2. abriré
   I will open
3. subiremos,
   we will go up
4. comprenderás
   you will understand
5. aprenderemos,
   we will learn
6. trabajarán
   they will work
7. Ud. correrá,
   you will run
8. contestarán,
   they will answer
9. trabajaré,
   I will work
10. prepararéis,
    you will prepare
11. pasaremos,
    we will spend
12. viajaré,
    I will travel
13. echarás,
    you will throw
14. partiré,
    I will leave
15. abriréis,
    you will open

16. Uds. escribirán,
    you will write
17. subiré,
    I will go up
18. comprenderá,
    she will understand
19. correremos,
    we will run
20. Ud. contestará,
    you will answer

21. tomaremos,
    we will take
22. enseñarán,
    they will teach
23. acabarás,
    you will finish
24. trabajará,
    he will work
25. escribiré
    I will write

Mastery Test

pp. 24–25

1. adornarás
2. admiraba
3. ofenderéis
4. molesta
5. Uds. discutirán
6. insistí
7. discutirá
8. emprenderemos
9. limpiarán
10. Uds. llaman
11. admiraré
12. adornó
13. molestas
14. discutiré
15. insistieron
16. cubrían
17. cubriremos
18. admiramos
19. Uds. emprendieron
20. insistimos

21. discutieron
22. limpiaremos
23. limpiaba
24. decidí
25. llama
26. ofendíamos
27. llamaremos
28. Ud. discutió
29. no admiraremos
30. no llaman
31. decidís
32. cubrí
33. Ud. no discutirá
34. no decidiremos
35. ¿limpiarás?
36. no insistiréis
37. cubrirán
38. Uds. limpiaron
39. insistíamos
40. ofendió

CONDITIONAL

Para practicar

pp. 26–28

admiraría, decidiría, trabajaría, viviría, bebería, abriría, moriría.

adornarías, ofenderías, responderías, estudiarías, venderías, escribirías, sentirías.

molestaría, emprendería, correría, necesitaría, aprendería, llevaría, partiría.

Para practicar (*cont.*)

llamaría, echaría, aprendería, contestaría, temería, sacaría, hablaría.

limpiaríamos, viajaríamos, comprenderíamos, preguntaríamos, leeríamos, tocaríamos, comeríamos.

cubriríais, pasaríais, subiríais, enseñaríais, creeríais, conoceríais, meteríais.

discutirían, guardarían, abrirían, escucharían, recibirían, traerían, pedirían.

insistirían, prepararían, escribirían, tomarían, asistirían, dormirían, rogarían.

Aplicación

pp. 28–29

A.
1. admirarían
2. discutiría
3. cubrirías
4. limpiaría
5. venderíais
6. preguntaría
7. venderían
8. estudiaríamos
9. viviríamos
10. temería
11. abriría
12. tomarían
13. escribiríamos
14. contestarían
15. temerían
16. llevarías
17. bebería
18. aprendería
19. echaría
20. viajarían
21. necesitaríais
22. escucharían
23. enseñaríamos
24. asistirían
25. recibirías

B. a)
1. contestaríamos, we should answer
2. aprendería, I should learn
3. escucharían, they should listen
4. leería, he should read
5. esconderíamos, we should hide
6. escribiríais, you should write
7. estudiarían, you should study
8. vendería, I should sell
9. enseñaría, she should teach
10. comprenderían, they should understand

b)
1. vivirían, you should live
2. abriría, he should open
3. trabajarían, they should work
4. subiríamos, we should go up
5. comprendería, he should understand
6. aprenderíais, you should learn
7. correría, he should run
8. prepararías, you should prepare
9. guardaríamos, we should keep
10. viajaría, she should travel

Mastery Test

pp. 29–30

1. decidirás
2. molestaría
3. Ud. adornaba
4. ¿ofendería?
5. insistí
6. discutiríamos
7. admiraron
8. no adornaría
9. ofenderé
10. ofendían
11. ¿limpiaría?
12. emprenden

13. admirarían
14. limpiaré
15. Uds. molestarían
16. no cubriremos
17. cubre
18. decidirían
19. ¿admirarás?
20. admiramos
21. insistían

22. no insistiría
23. Uds. limpiaron
24. decidiría
25. insistirás
26. ¿llamarían?
27. cubriríais
28. molestaremos
29. no ofenderían
30. ¿decidiré?

PROGRESSIVE TENSES

Para practicar

pp. 26–28

admirando, adornando, subiendo, cubriendo, acabando, corriendo, respondiendo, tomando, sacando, decidiendo, dando.

estoy abriendo, estoy llevando, estoy perdiendo, estoy buscando, estoy estudiando, estoy bebiendo.

estás viviendo, estás aprendiendo, estás tomando, estás escribiendo, estás trabajando, estás enseñando.

están vendiendo, están abriendo, están contestando, están asistiendo, están escuchando, están entrando.

estamos recibiendo, estamos echando, estamos admirando, estamos pasando, estamos respondiendo, estamos corriendo.

Aplicación

pp. 32–33

A.
1. estaba llevando
2. estabas estudiando
3. estabais trabajando
4. estábamos subiendo
5. estaban corriendo
6. estaba escuchando
7. estaban jugando
8. estábamos escribiendo
9. estabas comiendo
10. estaba partiendo
11. estábamos tomando
12. estaban acabando
13. estaba respondiendo
14. estaban decidendo
15. estaba cubriendo

B.
1. están recibiendo
2. estábamos trabajando
3. estáis abriendo
4. estabais preguntando
5. no estaba escuchando
6. estamos viviendo
7. está bebiendo
8. estaban asistiendo
9. estás vendiendo
10. no estaba tomando
11. estaba enseñando
12. estáis contestando
13. está estudiando
14. no estaba comiendo
15. estoy aprendiendo

Mastery Test

pp. 33–34

1. admiraba,	estaba admirando
2. decides,	estás decidiendo
3. limpiaba,	estaba limpiando
4. insistían,	estaban insistiendo
5. no preparan,	no están preparando
6. Ud. llama,	Ud. está llamando
7. cubrían,	estaban cubriendo
8. ¿adornaban Uds.?,	¿estaban adornando Uds.?
9. bebe,	está bebiendo
10. vivíamos,	estábamos viviendo
11. no escribías,	no estabas escribiendo
12. paso,	estoy pasando
13. estudian,	están estudiando
14. pasábamos,	estábamos pasando
15. ¿subís?	¿estáis subiendo?
16. abría,	estaba abriendo
17. ¿corría?,	¿estaba corriendo?
18. no vivía,	no estaba viviendo
19. no escribimos,	no estamos escribiendo

Repaso (Future, conditional progressive)

pp. 34–35

1. Uds. asistirán	20. estaban limpiando
2. estaba admirando	21. no abriré
3. ofenderás	22. perderíais
4. molestaría	23. Ud. está llamando
5. estáis buscando	24. limpiará
6. Ud. no discutiría	25. enseñarás
7. estaba insistiendo	26. estáis trabajando
8. está estudiando	27. echará
9. subiré	28. estaba escribiendo
10. admiraría	29. están bebiendo
11. estaban respondiendo	30. admiraría
12. no está molestando	31. estábamos llamando
13. ¿discutirán?	32. estaba discutiendo
14. estaba trabajando	33. admiraré
15. no estás corriendo	34. Ud. molestaría
16. escuchará	35. pasarán
17. estaba entrando	36. Uds. escribirían
18. estamos pasando	37. estaban decidiendo
19. cubriríamos	38. responderá

PERFECT TENSES

pp. 36–37

tú habías hablado, Ud. había hablado, él había hablado, nosotros habíamos hablado, vosotros habíais hablado, Uds. habían hablado, ellos habían hablado.

yo habré comido, tú habrás comido, Ud. habrá comido, él habrá comido, nosotros habremos comido, vosotros habréis comido, Uds. habrán comido, ellos habrán comido.

I will have eaten, you will have eaten, he will have eaten, we will have eaten, you will have eaten, they will have eaten.

yo habría partido, tú habrías partido, Ud. habría partido, él habría partido, nosotros habríamos partido, vosotros habríais partido, Uds. habrían partido, ellos habrían partido.

I would have left, you would have left, he would have left, we would have left, you would have left, they would have left.

Para practicar

pp. 37–38

1. he aprendido,	había aprendido,	habré aprendido,	habría aprendido
2. han limpiado,	habían limpiado,	habrán limpiado,	habrían limpiado
3. ha vivido,	había vivido	habrá vivido,	habría vivido
4. hemos comprado,	habíamos comprado,	habremos comprado,	habríamos comprado
5. has asistido,	habías asistido,	habrás asistido,	habrías asistido
6. han vendido,	habían vendido,	habrán vendido,	habrían vendido
7. hemos tomado,	habíamos tomado,	habremos tomado,	habríamos tomado
8. ha aprendido,	había aprendido,	habrá aprendido,	habría aprendido
9. ha bebido,	había bebido,	habrá bebido,	habría bedido
10. ha contestado,	había contestado,	habrá contestado,	habría contestado
11. habéis recibido,	habíais recibido,	habréis recibido,	habríais recibido
12. han preparado,	habían preparado,	habrán preparado,	habrían preparado
13. hemos enseñado,	habíamos enseñado,	habremos enseñado,	habríamos enseñado
14. has temido,	habías temido,	habrás temido,	habrías temido
15. ha preguntado,	había preguntado,	habrá preguntado,	habría preguntado
16. han estudiado,	habían estudiado,	habrán estudiado,	habrían estudiado
17. ha pasado,	había pasado,	habrá pasado,	habría pasado
18. hemos subido,	habíamos subido,	habremos subido,	habríamos subido
19. han salido,	habían salido,	habrán salido,	habrían salido
20. has guardado,	habías guardado,	habrás guardado,	habrías guardado
21. he esperado,	había esperado,	habré esperado,	habría esperado
22. habéis trabajado,	habíais trabajado,	habréis trabajado,	habríais trabajado
23. han vivido,	habían vivido,	habrán vivido,	habrían vivido
24. ha partido,	había partido,	habrá partido,	habría partido
25. ha acabado,	había acabado,	habrá acabado,	habría acabado

Aplicación

p. 39

1. Ud. ha comprendido
2. habías vendido
3. habían escuchado
4. habrán subido
5. ha preguntado
6. Ud. habrá discutido
7. habían aprendido
8. Ud. había estudiado
9. has escrito
10. habremos guardado
11. habrían admirado
12. habréis echado
13. habías temido
14. he asistido
15. habíamos tomado
16. habrías preparado
17. había bebido
18. habremos vivido
19. hemos corrido
20. habrá viajado
21. habrías decidido
22. habíais contestado
23. habíais partido
24. habré limpiado
25. habríais molestado

Mastery Test

pp. 39−40

1. habré aprendido
2. había limpiado
3. hemos comprado
4. habían vivido
5. habría corrido
6. he preguntado
7. habrás recibido
8. habías temido
9. ha asistido
10. habrían vendido
11. habremos tomado
12. Ud. ha contestado
13. he necesitado
14. Uds. habrían preguntado
15. han pasado
16. habrás discutido
17. han recibido
18. habría decidido
19. habrán escuchado
20. habremos entrado
21. Ud. habría asistido
22. habíais comprendido
23. hemos vivido
24. Uds. habrán trabajado
25. había tomado

Repaso (Indicative tenses)

pp. 40−41

1. contestas
2. vivían
3. estaba abriendo
4. estáis vendiendo
5. admiraré
6. trabajaron
7. pregunta
8. Uds. no ofenderán
9. subíamos
10. no venden
11. molestaría
12. estaba comprendiendo
13. estudiamos
14. ¿estáis adornando?
15. Uds. estaban aprendiendo
16. no vivimos
17. Ud. discute
18. estaba corriendo

19. ¿necesita?
20. molestaron
21. no contestaron
22. teme
23. insistimos
24. trabajé
25. echaré
26. preparabais
27. abre
28. Ud. estaba admirando
29. guardaron
30. ofenderé
31. estábamos pasando
32. adornaría
33. limpiaremos
34. escribimos

35. estaban cubriendo
36. Uds. estaban echando
37. temerán
38. estaba viviendo
39. viajaba
40. estudias
41. Uds. están llamando
42. abriríais
43. bebo
44. estábamos insistiendo
45. escribías
46. ¿llamarán?
47. subí
48. no discutirían
49. comprendió
50. viven

PRESENT SUBJUNCTIVE

Para practicar

pp. 42–44

eche, aprenda, moleste, emprenda, comprenda, asista, viva.

viajes, comprendas, llames, estudies, bebas, abras, escribas.

pase, suba, limpie, necesite, venda, escriba, prepare.

guarde, abra, cubra, conteste, aprenda, llame, tome.

preparemos, escribamos, discutamos, preguntemos, temamos, trabajemos, unamos.

trabajéis, viváis, insistáis, enseñéis, leáis, paséis, temáis.

respondan, admiren, decidan, escuchen, vivan, guarden, viajen.

corran, adornen, ofendan, tomen, reciban, echen, suban.

Aplicación

p. 44

1. lleve
2. viva
3. escriban
4. trabajéis
5. lean
6. hable
7. Ud. estudie
8. llamemos
9. viajes
10. abra
11. creamos
12. mande
13. escribas

14. tomemos
15. comprendan
16. coma
17. vivas
18. asista
19. Ud. note
20. caminen
21. meta
22. observéis
23. partáis
24. andes
25. insistamos

Mastery Test

pp. 44—45

1. no comprenda
2. ¡corra! ¡corran!
3. pregunte
4. estudie
5. beban
6. venda
7. estudien
8. no venda
9. ¡beba! ¡beban!
10. comprendamos
11. reciba
12. vendan
13. estudiéis

14. ¡no preguntes!
15. no corramos
16. recibas
17. enseñe
18. comprendáis
19. llamemos
20. abra
21. ¡escriba! ¡escriban!
22. viaje
23. tomes
24. Ud. viva
25. insistamos

IMPERFECT SUBJUNCTIVE

Para practicar

pp. 46—47

temiera, asistiera, abriera, acabara, escuchara, necesitara.

estudiara, abriera, aprendiera, tuviera, hablara, enseñara.

comprendiéramos, comiéramos, entráramos, partiéramos, viviéramos, metiéramos.

partieses, preguntases, vivieses, vendieses, hablases, guardases.

enseñase, tomase, comiese, aprendiese, asistiese, pasase.

hablasen, contestasen, estudiasen, tomasen, leyesen, escribiesen.

Aplicación

pp. 47—48

A.
1. hablara, hablase
2. viviéramos, viviésemos
3. corriéramos, corriésemos
4. partieras, partieses
5. pasara, pasase
6. esperarais, esperaseis
7. acabaran, acabasen
8. caminara, caminase
9. comprendiera, comprendiese
10. tomaran, tomasen
11. escribiera, escribiese
12. amara, amase

B.
1. contestáramos, contestásemos
2. vendieras, vendieses
3. preguntara, preguntase
4. aprendiera, aprendiese
5. escucharan, escuchasen
6. Ud. escribiera, escribiese
7. aprendieran, aprendiesen
8. Ud. estudiara, estudiase
9. viviéramos, viviésemos
10. temiera, temiese
11. abriera, abriese
12. enseñaran, enseñasen

13. bebieras, bebieses
14. compráramos, comprásemos
15. subieran, subiesen

13. asistiera, asistiese
14. tomáramos, tomásemos
15. Uds. recibieran, recibiesen

Mastery Test

p. 48

1. enseñara, enseñase
2. vivieran, viviesen
3. subiéramos, subiésemos
4. no comprendiera, comprendiese
5. tomaran, tomasen
6. corriera, corriese
7. contestaras, contestases
8. trabajara, trabajase
9. no prepararais, preparaseis
10. Ud. estudiara, estudiase

11. guardaran, guardasen
12. no pasáramos, pasásemos
13. viajara, viajase
14. necesitaras, necesitases
15. no viviera, viviese
16. abrierais, abrieseis
17. escribiera, escribiese
18. Uds. respondieran, respondiesen
19. temiera, temiese
20. comieran, comiesen

PERFECT TENSES OF THE SUBJUNCTIVE

Para practicar

p. 50

haya estudiado, haya necesitado, haya viajado,
hayamos pasado, hayas tomado, hayan vendido,
hayáis asistido, hayan llamado, hubiera (hubiese) vivido, hubieran (hubiesen) guardado, hubieras (hubieses) caminado,
hubieran (hubiesen) bebido, hubiéramos (hubiésemos) echado,
hubierais (hubieseis) asistido, hubiera (hubiese) aprendido

Aplicación

pp. 50–51

1. haya escuchado
2. hubiéramos (hubiésemos) vivido
3. hubieran (hubiesen) guardado
4. hayan trabajado
5. hayamos comprendido
6. hubiéramos (hubiésemos) vivido
7. hubieras (hubieses) subido
8. haya comprendido
9. no hubiera (hubiese) tomado
10. Ud. haya corrido
11. hubieran (hubiesen) respondido
12. hayas preparado
13. hubierais (hubieseis) estudiado
14. hayamos pasado
15. hayáis viajado
16. Uds. hayan necesitado
17. haya subido
18. hubiera (hubiese) partido
19. no hayas aprendido
20. no haya contestado
21. hubieras (hubieses) temido
22. hubieran (hubiesen) asistido
23. no haya vivido
24. hubieras (hubieses) discutido
25. hayáis llamado

Mastery Test

p. 51

1. haya aprendido
2. hubiera (hubiese) tomado
3. hubiera (hubiese) limpiado
4. hayas trabajado
5. hayamos comprado
6. hubiéramos (hubiésemos) vivido
7. hubieran (hubiesen) recibido
8. hubierais (hubieses) comprendido
9. hubiera (hubiese) asistido
10. hayamos tomado
11. haya necesitado
12. Ud. hubiera (hubiese) preguntado
13. hayan vivido
14. hubiera (hubiese) corrido
15. hayamos entrado
16. hubiera (hubiese) preguntado
17. hayan escuchado
18. hayáis temido
19. haya decidido
20. Uds. hubieran (hubiesen) contestado

Repaso del subjuntivo

pp. 52–53

1. comprenda
2. hayáis bebido
3. hubiéramos (hubiésemos) comprendido
4. no reciba
5. enseñara (enseñase)
6. corriéramos (corriésemos)
7. Ud. hubiera (hubiese) recibido
8. comprendas
9. no comprendiéramos (comprendiésemos)
10. haya estudiado
11. no corriera (corriese)
12. hayamos enseñado
13. hayan vendido
14. hubieran (hubiesen) bebido
15. no haya recibido
16. hubiera (hubiese) recibido
17. comprendamos
18. haya bebido
19. ¡estudie!
20. hubiéramos (hubiésemos) recibido
21. venda
22. comprendieran, comprendiesen
23. hayamos estudiado
24. no estudiéis
25. estudiara, estudiase
26. haya preguntado
27. hayas vendido
28. hubierais (hubieseis) bebido
29. no hubiera (hubiese) enseñado
30. estudiemos
31. ¡no vendáis!
32. comprendiera, comprendiese
33. haya estudiado
34. hubiera (hubiese) bebido
35. hubieran (hubiesen) enseñado
36. no preguntemos
37. bebieran, bebiesen
38. ¡corran!
39. corrieran, corriesen
40. Uds. hayan estudiado

REFLEXIVE VERBS

pp. 54–55

te levantabas, Ud. se levantaba, él se levantaba, nosotros nos levantábamos, vosotros os levantabais, Uds. se levantaban, ellos se levantaban.

te levantaste, Ud. se levantó, él se levantó, nos levantamos, os levantasteis, Uds. se levantaron, ellos se levantaron.

te levantarás, Ud. se levantará, él se levantará, nos levantaremos, os levantaréis, Uds. se levantarán, ellos se levantarán.

te levantarías, Ud. se levantaría, él se levantaría, nos levantaríamos, os levantaríais, Uds. se levantarían, ellos se levantarían.

me estaba levantando, estaba levantándome; I was getting up

(1) me había levantado (2) me habré levantado (3) me habría levantado

(1) I had gotten up (2) I will have gotten up (3) I would have gotten up

te levantes, Ud. se levante, él se levante, nos levantemos, os levantéis, Uds. se levanten, ellos se levanten

te levantaras, se levantara, se levantara, nos levantáramos, os levantarais, Uds. se levantaran, ellos se levantaran

te levantases, se levantase, se levantase, nos levantásemos, os levantaseis, Uds, se levantasen, ellos se levantasen

PRESENT PERFECT

p. 56

me haya levantado, te hayas levantado, se haya levantado, se haya levantado

I may have gotten up, you may have gotten up, you may have gotten up, he may have gotten up

nos hubiésemos levantado, os hubieseis levantado, se hubiesen levantado, se hubiesen levantado

we might have gotten up, you might have gotten up, you might have gotten up, they might have gotten up

Aplicación

pp. 56–57

A.
1. os lavéis
2. se peinaban
3. se levantó
4. nos peinemos
5. nos levantábamos
6. se lavan
7. nos levantamos
8. se hayan peinado
9. te lavabas
10. me peiné
11. os levantáis

B.
1. se hayan levantado
2. nos hemos levantado
3. te has peinado
4. os habéis levantado
5. nos habremos peinado
6. me había peinado
7. se había levantado
8. nos habríamos levantado
9. se habían peinado
10. se haya lavado
11. os hayáis peinado

Aplicación (*cont.*)

12. te hubieras levantado
13. se peina
14. me lavaré
15. te peinarías

12. nos hayamos lavado
13. me haya levantado
14. se habrán levantado
15. me habré lavado

Mastery Test

pp. 57–58

1. se haya lavado
2. se estaban lavando (estaban lavándose)
3. se peinan
4. se lavara (lavase)
5. me había levantado
6. se levantaron
7. se habrán lavado
8. me estoy peinando (estoy peinándome)
9. se habrían levantado
10. me levantaba

11. me lavo
12. se levante
13. nos lavaremos
14. se ha lavado
15. nos peináramos (peinásemos)
16. se lavaron
17. me lavaría
18. se levantan
19. te lavaste
20. se hubieran (hubiesen) lavado

Repaso de verbos regulares

pp. 58–61

A.
1. acabamos
2. comprendisteis
3. ellos temían
4. necesitaremos
5. partiríais
6. estamos enseñando
7. partís
8. Uds. hablen
9. han enseñado
10. hayáis hablado
11. estaban lavándose
12. habíais vendido
13. ellos hubiesen asistido
14. bebierais
15. habrán preguntado

16. habríais tomado
17. escuchan
18. hemos estudiado
19. habréis temido
20. aprenderán
21. comprendáis
22. están viviendo
23. Uds. habían acabado
24. contestamos
25. Uds. vendiesen
26. habríamos partido
27. abríais
28. Uds. entrarían
29. estabais comiendo
30. Uds. hayan tomado

B.
1. I leave
2. you wrote
3. you will attend
4. they used to live
5. we would take
6. you taught

7. he is studying
8. we will fear
9. you were opening
10. she would sell
11. you have attended
12. you have eaten

13. they had understood
14. you are listening
15. we will have had
16. I had studied
17. I was getting up
18. you will have spoken
19. we might drink
20. you would have answered
21. you may eat

22. he may write
23. he may have washed
24. we might learn
25. you might have studied
26. you may have spoken
27. you might have eaten
28. they fear
29. you would have carried
30. you used to carry

C. 1. temen
2. hubiera (hubiese) partido
3. comías
4. hayamos hablado
5. ¿hablasteis?
6. partía
7. aprenderemos
8. tomaras (tomases)
9. no escribiría
10. comprendieron
11. estás contestando
12. habrían partido
13. estabais hablando
14. he estudiado
15. ¡no acabéis!
16. habían partido
17. habré enseñado
18. Ud. habrá vivido
19. estamos viviendo
20. Uds. habrían enseñado
21. temamos
22. no lees
23. vendiera (vendiese)
24. no hayáis comido
25. estaba vendiendo

26. no hubierais (hubieseis) escuchado
27. vendo
28. ¿leerás?
29. llevaban
30. escribiste
31. asistiréis
32. tomaríamos
33. no está estudiando
34. estabais abriendo
35. Ud. no ha asistido
36. había comprendido
37. llevarías
38. habrán estudiado
39. Uds. no habrían necesitado
40. ¡beban!
41. no asistiéramos (asistiésemos)
42. has vivido
43. haya acabado
44. Uds. hubieran (hubiesen) aprendido
45. ¿abrís?
46. temía
47. habías tomado
48. preguntaron
49. Ud. entrará
50. ¿leerías?

STEM-CHANGING VERBS—CLASS I

p. 63

(1) piense, peinses, piense, piense, pensemos, penséis, piensen, piensen,

(2) entienda, entiendas, entienda, entienda, entendamos, entendáis, entiendan, entiendan.

(1) cuento, cuentas, cuenta, cuenta, contamos, contáis, cuentan, cuentan,

(2) vuelvo, vuelves, vuelve, vuelve, volvemos, volvéis, vuelven, vuelven.

Para practicar

p. 64

A.

cierro, encuentro, muestro, pierdo, revuelvo, enciendo.

confiesan, se acuestan, mueven, devuelven, aciertan, acuerdan.

nos sentamos, contamos, mostramos, perdemos, devolvemos, entendemos.

B.

cuentes, pienses, muerdas, apruebes, devuelvas, entiendas.

cierren, encuentren, muestren, pierdan, muevan, enciendan.

entendáis, revolváis, mostréis, mováis, confeséis, acordéis.

Mastery Test

p. 65

A.
1. they go to bed
2. I agree
3. she returns
4. you may warm
5. we may show
6. you lose
7. you may stir (turnover)
8. you may light
9. he approved
10. I used to sit
11. it cost
12. it will snow
13. I confess
14. they give back
15. close

B.
1. perdisteis
2. entiendan
3. encontremos
4. ¿cierras?
5. no entiendes
6. movieron
7. estaba moviendo
8. muestren
9. mueves
10. calentamos
11. estoy encendiendo
12. no pierden
13. muerda
14. revuelvas
15. cuesta

STEM-CHANGING VERBS—CLASS II
Para practicar

pp. 67–68

adviertes, mientes, mueres, hieres, consientes

se divierta, sienta, duerma, mienta, muera

hirieron, advirtieron, se divirtieron, durmieron, consintieron

muriéramos (muriésemos), sintiéramos (sintiésemos), mintiéramos (mintiésemos), durmiéramos (durmiésemos), advirtiéramos (advirtiésemos)

muriendo, hiriendo, consintiendo, advirtiendo, divirtiéndose

Mastery Test

p. 68

A.
1. you used to lie
2. we sleep (slept)
3. she died
4. they might lie
5. he had felt
6. they have fun
7. he wounded
8. he may consent
9. I do not notice
10. you lied
11. I felt
12. you may die
13. you may feel
14. they may sleep
15. we may have fun

B.
1. no hieren
2. has dormido
3. consintamos
4. muriera (muriese)
5. duerma
6. te divertiste
7. mentiremos
8. estaban muriendo
9. estaba sintiendo
10. durmiera (durmiese)
11. consentiría
12. Ud. advirtió
13. duermo
14. sintieran (sintiesen)
15. os divirtáis

STEM-CHANGING VERBS-CLASS III

Para practicar

pp. 69–70

impide, compite, sirve, mide

gimáis, pidáis, impidáis, compitáis

se vistieron, sirvieron, midieron, impidieron.

Mastery Test

p. 70

1. they might groan
2. I may dress
3. he would ask for
4. we used to measure
5. you may measure
6. we prevent
7. you groaned
8. I will compete
9. we might serve
10. he groans
11. you measured
12. they served
13. I compete
14. they get dressed
15. you may prevent

Repaso (Stem-changing verbs)

pp. 70–71

A.

gime, compite, cierra, siente, impide, muestra, encuentra, se divierte, se sienta, revuelve.

B.

aprobemos, midamos, durmamos, confesemos, mintamos, advirtamos, pidamos, nos vistamos, repitamos, consintamos.

C.

1. entienden	16. muestres
2. consintamos	17. me divirtiera (divirtiese)
3. me vista	18. sirvieron
4. no se está divirtiendo (no está divirtiéndose)	19. no perdéis
5. cerremos	20. duerma
6. pediste	21. impide
7. no advirtió	22. devuelva
8. encuentra	23. sintieron
9. Ud. gimiera	24. Uds. impidan
10. muera	25. ¿entiende?
11. muevas	26. no están muriendo (no mueren)
12. sirviéramos (sirviésemos)	27. no compitió
13. advierten	28. nieve
14. cierro	29. estás mintiendo (mientes)
15. compite	30. pidieran (pidiesen)

ORTHOGRAPHIC CHANGES

Para practicar

pp. 74–75

seques, coloques, obligues, entregues, amenaces, analices, averigües, mengües.

alcancen, abracen, lleguen, castiguen, arriesguen, rasquen, repliquen, expliquen.

expliqué, saqué, indiqué, negué, llegué, castigué, rogué, repliqué, empecé, crucé, rechacé, almorcé, marqué, apacigüé, santigüé.

Mastery Test

pp. 75–76

A.		B.	
1. he may explain		1. apacigüemos	
2. you might mark		2. pagué	
3. I may turn off		3. saquen	
4. I embraced		4. no averigüé	
5. I handed over		5. castigues	
6. we may stumble		6. no coloque	
7. they may dry		7. arriesgué	
8. you may punish		8. fatiguemos	
9. you may reject		9. no replique	
10. you may find out		10. cruces	
11. you may reply		11. roguéis	
12. we may load		12. indiqué	
13. you may threaten		13. reza	
14. I decreased		14. lances	
15. I took out		15. lleguen	
16. we may bless		16. no expliqué	
17. he may arrive		17. no analicemos	
18. you may analyze		18. repliquéis	
19. they may pacify		19. lancé	
20. he may reach (achieve)		20. sollocé	

Para practicar

p. 78

encojo, dirijo, cojo, exijo, ejerzo, convenzo, esparzo, extingo, delinco, acojo.

extingamos, delincamos, distingamos, escojamos, infligamos, finjamos, cojamos, esparzamos, ejerzamos, dirijamos.

Aplicación

p. 79

1. I exercise
2. you convinced
3. I will scatter
4. you used to welcome
5. they may distinguish
6. we may pretend
7. you have convinced
8. I will direct
9. he would follow
10. you may extinguish
11. you used to exercise
12. I demand
13. I followed
14. you extinguished
15. they may convince
16. I pretended
17. he broke the law
18. they may catch (seize)
19. I extinguish
20. you may break the law

Mastery Test

pp. 79—80

1. vencieras (vencieses)
2. inflija
3. distingo
4. ejercimos
5. no exijo
6. no distingas
7. no convencerá
8. ¿escogerán Uds? (¿elegirán Uds.?)
9. no extingamos
10. esparcí
11. dirigimos
12. distinguió
13. delinco
14. ejerces
15. acoja
16. extingan
17. no convenzan
18. finjo
19. distinguiréis
20. no delincas

Para practicar

p. 82

aparezcas, ofrezcas, merezcas, reconozcas, compadezcas, confíes, guíes, descontinúes.

desafío, parezco, obedezco, agradezco, insinúo, desconfío.

leyeron, poseyeron, enviaron, continuaron, conocieron, ofrecieron.

Aplicación

p. 83

1. estamos leyendo
2. enviáis
3. continuéis
4. ofrecemos
5. Uds. desafíen
6. aborrezcáis
7. merezcamos
8. Uds. aparezcan
9. guiamos
10. desconocieron
11. poseyeron
12. Uds. insinúen
13. se enriquezcan
14. parecimos
15. nos habituamos
16. creyésemos
17. Uds. complacían
18. ellas desconfían
19. descontinuamos
20. reconocemos

Mastery Test

pp. 83–84

1. ¿leyó?
2. desaparezcamos
3. continúe
4. envíen
5. poseía
6. Ud. no conozca
7. desconfiemos
8. no guío
9. leyeras
10. compadezca
11. enviaba
12. descontinúes
13. creíamos
14. desaparecéis
15. enviaron
16. no creyó
17. aborrecí
18. ¿confías?
19. conozcan
20. continuó

ORTHOGRAPHIC STEM CHANGES

Para practicar

pp. 87–89

corrijo, ruego, ciego, tropiezo, consigo, construyo, sonrío.

niega, persigue, ríe, destruye, se esfuerza, elige, juega.

colegí, rogué, almorcé, incluí, reí, proseguí, cegué.

corrigieron, consiguieron, sonrieron, restituyeron, eligieron, instruyeron, negaron.

ciegues, juegues, tropieces, corrijas, prosigas, destruyas, rías.

neguemos, nos esforcemos, elijamos, consigamos, sonriamos, concluyamos, juguemos.

corrigiera (corrigiese), prosiguiera (prosiguiese), riera (riese), construyera (construyese), eligiera (eligiese), constituyera (constituyese), consiguiera (consiguiese).

coligiendo, colgando, almorzando, sonriendo, destruyendo, persiguiendo.

cegado, empezado, elegido, seguido, reído, concluido, huido.

Aplicación

pp. 89–90

1. rueguen Uds.
2. tropezamos
3. ellos almuercen
4. cegamos
5. escogemos
6. empezamos
7. juegan
8. nos esforzamos
9. colguéis
10. empezamos
11. huyen
12. Uds. sonrieron
13. ellos destruyeron
14. concluyésemos
15. habéis huido
16. ellos corrijan
17. Uds. consiguieron
18. seguimos
19. escogiéramos
20. consigáis
21. estaban siguiendo
22. elijamos
23. corregimos
24. persiguen
25. incluyáis
26. concluíamos
27. Uds. habían reído
28. instruímos
29. Uds. han restituido
30. están sonriendo

Mastery Test

pp. 90–91

A.
1. I may turn off
2. I exercise
3. you send
4. I stumble
5. extinguish!
6. I offer
7. I handed over
8. they may distinguish
9. you may be unacquainted
10. I played
11. we may pretend
12. I guide
13. you may eat lunch
14. I correct
15. he possessed
16. you may reply
17. they may catch
18. you may insinuate
19. you may threaten
20. I demand
21. I might believe
22. I marked
23. you may get
24. I smile
25. you may beg
26. they may convince
27. you might conclude
28. you may pacify
29. you may break the law
30. he destroyed

B.
1. pagué
2. escogiera (escogiese); eligiera (eligiese)
3. ¿leyó?
4. no averigüé
5. siguieron
6. continúe
7. no coloque
8. no extingas
9. envíen
10. lleguemos
11. ¿consiguió Ud.?
12. no conozcas
13. Ud. cruce
14. sigo
15. no guío
16. rogué
17. delinco
18. leyeras (leyeses)
19. empecéis
20. dirija
21. destruyeron
22. no expliqué
23. finjo
24. no te ríes
25. Ud. replique
26. no convenzan
27. creíamos
28. lancé
29. escojas (elijas)
30. concluyéramos (concluyésemos)

Repaso general 1

pp. 92–93

A.
1. partimos
2. comprendisteis
3. vivían
4. asistiremos
5. tomaríais
6. estamos escribiendo
7. estaban vistiéndose
8. hemos hablado
9. Uds. habían vendido
10. habréis asistido
11. habrían bebido
12. contesten Uds.
13. aprendierais
14. hayan entrado
15. hubiéramos tomado
16. acordamos
17. se acuesten
18. consintamos
19. no se diviertan
20. Uds. pidieron
21. leyeron
22. reímos
23. negamos
24. Uds. incluyan
25. juguéis
26. reconocemos
27. Uds. persiguieron
28. almorcéis
29. averigüemos
30. distinguimos

B.
1. temen
2. bebías
3. mostréis
4. empecé
5. ¿hablaste?
6. sirvieron
7. creíamos
8. leyerais
9. no escribiría
10. advierte
11. no convenzan
12. no empiece
13. hablabas
14. nieva
15. Uds. expliquen
16. dirijáis
17. habré enseñado
18. pidieran
19. no te ríes
20. no guío
21. temamos
22. escojo
23. ¿continúas?
24. no expliqué
25. vendía
26. rogué
27. destruyeron
28. escojas
29. llevaban
30. envía

Repaso general 2

pp. 93–95

A.
1. había temido
2. he partido
3. habían vivido
4. habré necesitado
5. habríamos partido
6. hayas comido
7. hubiésemos vendido
8. Ud. había reído
9. has restituido
10. han enviado
11. he descontinuado
12. he obedecido

B.
1. habrían partido
2. lean
3. concluyéramos (concluyésemos)
4. no está estudiando
5. comprenden
6. pagué
7. cruces
8. Ud. llevaría
9. cerremos
10. escogiera (escogiese); eligiera (eligiese)
11. ¿conseguiste?
12. no asistiéramos (asistiésemos)

13. había creído
14. hayan desaparecido
15. yo hubiera poseído
16. ha tropezado
17. haya distinguido
18. han jugado
19. hayan explicado
20. he conseguido
21. había herido
22. has elegido
23. él haya delinquido
24. han sonreído
25. habían destruido
26. habréis hablado
27. había aprendido
28. había dormido
29. hubiéramos corregido
30. hubiera huido

13. impidierais (impidieseis)
14. ¿leyó?
15. lleguemos
16. ¿abre Ud.?
17. impidieron
18. no averigüé
19. no cruzáis
20. entrarás
21. me visto
22. siguieron
23. cierro
24. ¿leerían Uds.?
25. mueran
26. ¡continúen!
27. sigo
28. Uds. habrán vivido
29. perdáis
30. no busque

IRREGULAR VERBS

Para practicar

pp. 97–98

desasgo, quepo, ando, decaigo

asen, andan, caen, caben

desasió, cupo, anduvo, cayó

asiremos, decaeremos, cabremos, andaremos

desasgas, caigas, quepas, andes

decayerais (decayeseis), anduvierais (anduvieseis), cupierais (cupieseis), asierais (asieseis)

Aplicación

p. 98

1. they would fall
2. we will fit
3. you may have fallen
4. you were walking
5. you would fit
6. they fell
7. you would decline
8. you fitted
9. we loosen
10. we walked
11. we may decline
12. they may fit
13. you may fall
14. I will seize
15. we declined

16. he will fall
17. I might fit
18. I fall
19. I fit
20. they may seize
21. you might decline
22. we will walk
23. they might have seized
24. they would have walked
25. you will loosen
26. they are declining
27. we may walk
28. he will have declined
29. they might walk
30. you seize

Mastery Test

pp. 99–100

1. no caerían
2. hubiera (hubiese) andado
3. asirían
4. ¿andabas?
5. decaen
6. desasieran (desasiesen)
7. decaeríais
8. ¿andaré?
9. desasgo
10. anduvo
11. ¿cupo?
12. desasíamos
13. decayeron
14. habríamos cabido
15. no caeré
16. cabe
17. anduviéramos (anduviésemos)
18. había asido
19. no habría caído
20. ande
21. habías asido
22. ando
23. Uds. caerían
24. ¿asió?
25. ha caído
26. quepamos
27. andabas
28. caíamos
29. hayas andado
30. habíamos cabido
31. haya asido
32. caísteis
33. hubiera (hubiese) caído
34. Ud. cupo
35. cupiera (cupiese)
36. decaes
37. asgan
38. cayéramos (cayésemos)
39. no quepa
40. caigáis

Para practicar

p. 101

deduzco, maldigo, yerro, doy, traduzco.

produjeron, bendijeron, dieron, condujeron, erraron.

traducirá, maldecirá, deducirá, bendecirá, dará.

habían dado, habían deducido, habían bendecido, habían errado, habían dicho.

des, produzcas, bendigas, yerres, digas.

erráramos (errásemos), tradujéramos (tradujésemos), maldijéramos (maldijésemos), diéramos (diésemos), condujéramos (condujésemos).

Aplicación

pp. 102–03

1. you deduced
2. you give
3. he will say
4. we may wander
5. we used to lead
6. they may give
7. we may say
8. you were cursing
9. he translates
10. you would have given
11. they said
12. I may have said

13. she led
14. I give
15. you may wander
16. we would say
17. I may deduce
18. you gave
19. they bless
20. you wander
21. he would produce

22. you might give
23. he might say
24. I wander
25. she might translate
26. we were giving
27. they would have cursed
28. I wandered
29. I produce
30. I will give

Mastery Test

pp. 103–04

1. dirás
2. conducís
3. erremos
4. haya dicho
5. no daba
6. tradujiste
7. bendijera
8. daremos
9. Uds. produzcan
10. ¿condujo?
11. no dijerais
12. ¿da?
13. yerro
14. dedujera (dedujese)
15. maldeciríamos
16. dieron
17. produjera (produjese)
18. ¡no traduzcan!
19. ¿están diciendo?
20. erraron

21. hubieran (hubiesen) dado
22. ¿no habéis dicho?
23. produzco
24. yerra
25. no diremos
26. no decían
27. no doy
28. deduzca
29. no traduzcan
30. maldijiste
31. ¿disteis?
32. conduciremos
33. Ud. dé
34. bendigo
35. produjeron
36. traducías
37. no diera
38. maldiga
39. hayan dado
40. no conduzca

Para practicar

pp. 105–06

1. vamos
2. Uds. satisfagan
3. habrán
4. estamos
5. ibais
6. nosotros hubiéramos
7. hemos
8. estuvieron
9. fuimos
10. harán

11. hubisteis
12. hicierais
13. ellos vayan
14. estuvierais
15. habéis hecho
16. Uds. hayan
17. fuerais
18. satisficieron
19. Uds. estén
20. satisfacemos

Aplicación

p. 106

1. he will have satisfied
2. we are
3. there is (are)
4. you went
5. he would do
6. you satisfied
7. there would have been
8. you may have done
9. I would not be
10. I will satisfy
11. they had
12. we used to do (make)
13. you were going
14. we might satisfy
15. there may have been
16. I would have been
17. you may satisfy
18. you might be
19. you would have
20. we did
21. they were
22. he might do
23. he has
24. you may not go
25. I would have done
26. you were satisfying
27. we might go
28. they may be
29. I was
30. he goes

Mastery Test

pp. 107–08

1. hubiéramos (hubiésemos) ido
2. estuve
3. haya hecho
4. habrían satisfecho
5. estaba
6. no habrán ido
7. no hacíamos
8. Uds. satisfarán
9. estamos
10. había hecho
11. iba
12. satisfice
13. estemos
14. no hay
15. no satisfacemos
16. ¿va?
17. Ud. estará
18. hicieron
19. satisfagamos
20. no estuviera (estuviese)
21. habría habido
22. fueras
23. satisfacía
24. habrá
25. vaya
26. hubiera (hubiese) habido
27. satisfaga
28. harás
29. hubiera (hubiese)
30. hubieran (hubiesen) estado
31. fuisteis
32. ha habido
33. no hagan
34. satisfago
35. hubieran (hubiesen) hecho
36. no iré
37. haya
38. haríamos
39. había
40. no estoy

Para practicar

pp. 109–10

propones, hueles, puedes, oyes, compones.

dispusieron, pudieron, oyeron, impusieron, supusieron.

dispondré, expondré, impondré, propondré, supondré.

componga, pueda, oiga, huela, exponga.

hayamos oído, hayamos dispuesto, hayamos puesto, hayamos supuesto, hayamos podido.

Aplicación

p. 110

1. pusieran
2. podamos
3. oirían
4. pudisteis
5. disponéis
6. oíamos
7. Uds. podrán
8. olieron
9. hemos compuesto
10. habremos podido
11. oiremos
12. oleríais
13. impondrían
14. podían
15. habrán oído

16. huelen
17. expongamos
18. oyeron
19. pudiéramos
20. hayamos propuesto
21. podríais
22. oigáis
23. olemos
24. supondréis
25. podéis
26. Uds. oyen
27. oláis
28. dispusieron
29. oliéramos
30. hubierais puesto

Mastery Test

p. 111

1. oíste
2. no habíamos podido
3. huela
4. no habría puesto
5. no estabais oyendo (no oíais)
6. están imponiendo
7. pude
8. ¿huele?
9. oirían
10. pueda
11. habré compuesto
12. ¿pone?
13. ¿oye?
14. no expondrás
15. propongan

16. no pudiera (pudiese)
17. hubiéramos (hubiésemos) oído
18. Uds. podrían
19. olieran (oliesen)
20. supongamos
21. no oiréis
22. ¿puedes?
23. dispusiéramos (dispusiésemos)
24. no pondrán
25. oyeron
26. pudisteis
27. suponía
28. podrás
29. no oyéramos (oyésemos)
30. ¿expusisteis?

184

Aplicación

pp. 113–14

A.
1. fuimos (éramos)
2. supieras (supieses)
3. salimos (salíamos)
4. supo (sabía)
5. fuiste (eras)
6. saliera (saliese)
7. fuera (fuese)
8. fui (era)
9. quisimos (queríamos)
10. salí (salía)
11. había sabido
12. habíais salido
13. quiso (quería)
14. estabas saliendo
15. quisieran (quisiesen)

B.
1. salíamos
2. Uds. sabrán
3. querréis
4. salieron
5. sepáis
6. saldríais
7. saben
8. sois
9. habíamos querido
10. salgan
11. serán
12. quisieran
13. saldremos
14. seamos
15. Uds. fueran

C.
1. we would be
2. we were
3. you wanted
4. I will have been
5. you might be
6. I have known
7. we will have known
8. we may want
9. you will know
10. you were
11. he knew
12. he had gone out
13. they were wanting
14. you would know
15. they may have left
16. we might have known
17. I may be
18. he might want
19. they might leave
20. we might know

Mastery Test

pp. 114–15

1. supiera
2. habéis salido
3. querría
4. no fui
5. habéis sabido
6. somos
7. salga
8. querrás
9. sabíamos
10. era
11. queríamos
12. no saliéramos (saliésemos)
13. sabréis
14. sean
15. haya querido
16. Ud. no será
17. habrán sabido
18. salieron
19. habías querido
20. no salimos
21. haya sabido
22. ¿es?
23. salías
24. no quise
25. habrían sabido
26. ¿no quieren?
27. hemos sido
28. saldrá
29. sabríamos
30. Uds. quisieran (quisiesen)

31. salgo
32. Ud. supo
33. he querido
34. hubiéramos (hubiésemos) sido
35. quieras

36. ¿saldrían?
37. sé
38. fuera (fuese)
39. fueron
40. habremos sido

Para practicar

p. 117

contraigo, convengo, detengo, mantengo, sostengo.

mantiene, viene, vale, retiene, trae.

convendrán, detendrán, mantendrán, valdrán,
sostendrán.

contuvo, trajo, convino, sostuvo, detuvo.

vengas, mantengas, contraigas, contengas, valgas.

contrajéramos (contrajésemos), viniéramos
(viniésemos), tuviéramos (tuviésemos), sostuviéramos (sostuviésemos), mantuviéramos (mantuviésemos).

Aplicación

p. 118

1. he will have come
2. you may have brought
3. they had
4. we may be worth
5. they will bring
6. I had
7. we would be worth
8. they had come
9. we used to have
10. you would bring
11. you have been worth
12. you come
13. you will be worth
14. he might come
15. I brought
16. I will have
17. he might be worth
18. they might have
19. he has brought
20. they may come
21. they used to bring
22. you would have
23. we used to be worth
24. we will have come
25. you may bring
26. you have
27. I would be worth
28. you might have
29. we might bring
30. you were coming

186

Mastery Test

pp. 118–19

1. no ha vendio
2. había tenido
3. trajeras
4. valió
5. hubiéramos (hubiésemos) tenido
6. habían traido
7. vinisteis
8. traía
9. tuvo
10. valen
11. no tendrían
12. trajo
13. venían
14. ¿tienes?
15. traigan
16. venga
17. no estamos trayendo
18. tendremos
19. valdrás
20. ¿tenéis?
21. no traigas
22. vengo
23. Uds. tengan
24. no valgo
25. hayas venido
26. no traería
27. tuvieron
28. trajeron
29. ¿vendrán?
30. tuvierais
31. valiera (valiese)
32. tenías
33. traigamos
34. ha tenido
35. has traído
36. ¿no tuvieron?
37. no valdría
38. estáis trayendo
39. viniéramos (viniésemos)
40. trajera

IRREGULAR PAST PARTICIPLES

Aplicación

p. 120

1. I may see
2. they might have discovered
3. we might see
4. you may have seen
5. you would see
6. we saw
7. we have described
8. he may see
9. he will have died
10. you were seeing
11. you will see
12. I had resolved
13. we see
14. you saw
15. they would have returned

Mastery Test

pp. 120–21

1. no vemos
2. veían
3. vierais (vieseis)
4. no había escrito
5. veas
6. no vio
7. ¿han descubierto?
8. hubiera visto
9. veríamos
10. no ha cubierto
11. veía
12. no verá
13. haya visto
14. habrían abierto
15. ¿no veis?

Repaso de verbos irregulares

pp. 121–23

A.
1. he will have come
2. you had
3. they would go
4. you will say
5. you went (were)
6. he would want
7. we see
8. I was (went)
9. I brought
10. he was going out
11. you will have known
12. they might be
13. we had been able
14. I would have put
15. they may give
16. I may walk
17. they might fall
18. we may be worth
19. he had fitted
20. you heard
21. he will have satisfied
22. he would not do
23. we lead
24. you would seize
25. you used to translate

26. there may have been
27. she says
28. we go
29. we had been
30. you will have
31. they used to come
32. they may have seen
33. you wanted
34. he used to bring
35. they gave
36. you may be
37. you used to go out
38. you used to put
39. we can
40. we will know
41. we had heard
42. you will have been worth
43. I may have done
44. you will satisfy
45. I will fall
46. she walked
47. he may fit
48. there will be
49. they translated
50. I may lead

B.
1. sean
2. habremos venido
3. decías
4. ¿va?
5. viéramos (viésemos)
6. tuvieran (tuviesen)
7. habías querido
8. traería
9. sepa
10. estamos
11. habrás puesto
12. podía
13. no hemos dado
14. no salió
15. hayáis caído
16. oíamos
17. cayó
18. valdríamos
19. anduvo
20. cupe
21. no haré
22. traducían
23. habrían asido
24. condujo
25. deduzcas

26. habría
27. habrá dicho
28. iría
29. hayan visto
30. tengan
31. venía
32. quería
33. habéis sido
34. no traigamos
35. no sabe
36. pudiste
37. estaremos
38. ¡den!
39. saldría
40. pondréis
41. oiga
42. no andaremos
43. cabré
44. Ud. ha valido
45. satisficiéramos (satisficiésemos)
46. no hicimos
47. caigo
48. asgamos
49. hubieran (hubiesen) sido
50. condujera (condujese)

Repaso general 2

pp. 123–25

A.
1. we think
2. you opened
3. they may lose
4. she answers
5. I understand
6. I arrived
7. you will say
8. he had fun
9. I sleep
10. we brought
11. I did
12. they will come
13. you may know
14. I might put
15. we may be able
16. you may choose
17. we might return
18. they may take out
19. they distinguish
20. I might look for
21. I will read
22. you would know
23. they will have
24. I gave
25. you will see
26. he insinuates
27. I may begin
28. we send (sent)
29. I may have played
30. I may trust

B.
1. escribíamos
2. entiende
3. viven
4. viajaban (estaban viajando)
5. guardas
6. traían (estaban trayendo)
7. ¿decimos?
8. quiere
9. se vistió
10. no vieron
11. salimos
12. pusiera (pusiese)
13. no han hecho
14. no sé
15. pudiste
16. dirigimos
17. busqué
18. escogieran (escogiesen), eligieran (eligiesen)
19. ¡expliquen!
20. llegue
21. vales
22. ¿leyeron?
23. dieras (dieses)
24. no vayamos
25. tenga
26. jueguen
27. negué
28. continúe
29. no empecé
30. envíen

Repaso general 3

pp. 125–26

A.
1. I began
2. I may play
3. we were denying
4. she continues
5. they will send
6. you get
7. I had
8. you led
9. I was going out
10. they knew (found out)

11. he would hear
12. you fit
13. he may put
14. we would be able
15. I come
16. they will have died
17. I was laughing
18. he was contributing
19. he destroys
20. you used to possess

21. they may construct
22. he loses
23. we were serving.
24. he used to know
25. she wounded
26. I may think
27. they threw
28. he will have lost
29. you were listening
30. she had returned

B.
1. jugabais
2. empezaran (empezasen)
3. continúo
4. confié
5. no leen
6. no quiso
7. serían
8. no corrijo
9. fui
10. dijo
11. vea
12. Ud. caía
13. hice
14. he puesto
15. saldrán

16. lea
17. habíamos dormido
18. riéramos (riésemos)
19. muera
20. no creyeron
21. envie
22. ¿consentís?
23. destruyan
24. repetía
25. perdíamos
26. no vuelves (devuelves)
27. pasábamos
28. vivía
29. entendisteis
30. han abierto

FINAL REVIEW

Para practicar 1

pp. 132–33

1. aprendo, aprendía, aprendí
2. zurce, zurcía, zurció
3. peca, pecaba, pecó
4. avergonzamos, avergonzábamos, avergonzamos
5. os erguís, os erguíais, os erguisteis
6. sollozas, sollozabas, sollozaste
7. se visten, se vestían, se vistieron
8. caben, cabían, cupieron
9. huele, olía, olió
10. yazgo, yacía, yací
11. expone, exponía, expuso
12. apaciguan, apaciguaban, apaciguaron

13. te gradúas, te graduabas, te graduaste
14. roo, roía, roí
15. se enoja, se enojaba, se enojó
16. poseemos, poseíamos, poseímos
17. almuerzas, almorzabas, almorzaste
18. revuelven, revolvían, revolvieron
19. huye, huía, huyó
20. salgo, salía, salí
21. desniegan, desnegaban, desnegaron
22. suponéis, suponíais, supusisteis
23. se levanta, se levantaba, se levantó
24. compadecemos, compadecíamos, compadecimos
25. ahogas, ahogabas, ahogaste

Para practicar 2

p. 133

A.
1. vamos
2. habéis estado
3. ellos arriesgarían
4. ellas habían querido
5. se divirtieron
6. os levantasteis
7. hubieran escuchado
8. estamos traduciendo
9. hayamos fregado
10. dormiríais

B.
1. hubiera avergonzado
2. habías tomado
3. habría hablado
4. habrá dormido
5. no haya desconfiado
6. he estado comiendo
7. había dicho
8. hubiese sentido
9. habré olido
10. hubieses vestido

Para practicar 3

p. 134

A.
1. he estudiado
2. ha necesitado
3. hemos contado
4. habéis ofendido
5. han dicho
6. has sido
7. he molido
8. ha supuesto
9. han dormido
10. habéis descrito

B.
1. complacería
2. ofenderíais
3. dirías
4. sostendrían
5. se entrenaría
6. nos meceríamos
7. extinguiría
8. sabrían
9. venderían
10. ¿acertaría?

Para practicar 4

pp. 134–35

A.
1. escuchando
2. careciendo
3. midiendo
4. estando
5. siendo
6. persiguiendo
7. advirtiendo
8. vistiéndose
9. sirviendo
10. huyendo

B.
1. abierto
2. ejercido
3. supuesto
4. revuelto
5. hecho
6. descubierto
7. agradecido
8. satisfecho
9. costado
10. vuelto

Para practicar 5

pp. 135–36

A.

sirve, influye, vive, decae, huele.

B.

reñí, sonreí, seguí, contraje, resolví.

C.

comprendáis, convengáis, encontréis, insinuéis, repitáis.

D.

habrá muerto, habrá perdido, habrá escrito, habrá propuesto, habrá cabido.

E.

oíamos, nos enriquecíamos, desconocíamos, negábamos, uníamos.

Para practicar 6

p. 136

rasques, asgas, friegues, tuerzas, cargues.

escuchemos, conduzcamos, descontinuemos, destruyamos, neguemos.

contraiga, crea, delinca, valga, conteste.

sequéis, gimáis, os habituéis, aborrezcáis, escondáis.

duerma, surja, impida, prepare, diga.

Aplicación 1

p. 137

1. I may have
2. Juan and Pedro may enjoy themselves
3. you had gone out
4. they were consenting
5. I will have written
6. he would speak
7. you had revolved
8. they measured
9. I used to notice
10. you might feel
11. you might have moved
12. when will you begin?
13. come!
14. you might have enjoyed yourself
15. she would have believed
16. you may not trust! (do not trust!)
17. are you going to play?
18. we will dry
19. I was cleaning
20. she needed
21. we would be able
22. you offended

23. you may find
24. Juan used to laugh
25. you had
26. we used to dress
27. he will have sobbed
28. he had
29. we were studying

30. we had not found
31. we might sleep
32. you may have travelled
33. you would know
34. they need
35. I might measure

Aplicación 2

pp. 138

1. dormimos (dormíamos)
2. influyeras (influyeses)
3. abrió (abría)
4. había revuelto
5. habíais elegido
6. rogaron (rogaban)
7. desconocisteis (desconocíais)
8. no bebiesen
9. fuimos (éramos)
10. pasamos (pasábamos)
11. encontramos (encontrábamos)
12. expusiera
13. se enriqueciesen

14. creímos (creíamos)
15. habíais aceptado
16. cargasen
17. fueron (eran)
18. distinguisteis (distinguíais)
19. habíamos convocado
20. compitieras
21. estaban corriendo
22. obedeciésemos
23. finjierais (finjieseis)
24. estuvieron (estaban)
25. aborrecimos (aborrecíamos)

Aplicación 3

pp. 138–39

1. estamos oliendo
2. vivimos
3. admirábamos
4. merecían
5. hayáis desaparecido
6. habrían ejercido
7. obliguéis
8. gemiréis
9. compusieran
10. aprenderíamos
11. riñeron
12. hayan conseguido
13. ¡corran!

14. habríamos pensado
15. huyáis
16. nos estamos habituando a
17. han
18. habéis colgado
19. hubierais desconfiado
20. no esparzáis
21. pecaremos
22. sonreísteis
23. hayan dormido
24. nos sentaríamos
25. habíais erguido

Aplicación 4

p. 139

1. haya hablado
2. habían comido
3. habíais estado
4. habrán pasado
5. no hubierais confiado
6. hayas extinguido
7. habremos movido
8. hayan molido
9. hayáis sentido
10. hayamos perseguido
11. habrás entrado
12. hubieses carecido
13. te habrás enriquecido
14. han ofrecido
15. habrías decaído
16. habrá sido
17. habríais colocado
18. había huido
19. he influido
20. hubieran acordado
21. habías aprobado
22. habrías asistido
23. habréis llegado
24. hubieseis delinquido
25. había reído

Aplicación 5

p. 140

1. necesitáramos (necesitásemos)
2. rogase
3. pagaras
4. preparaseis
5. pusiese
6. produjera
7. Pedro y Elena abriesen
8. apaciguara
9. impidiesen
10. mecieran
11. compadecieseis
12. prosiguieras
13. pagasen
14. complaciera
15. jugásemos
16. tuviera
17. colocase
18. apagaras
19. emprendiesemos
20. tomara
21. repitieseis
22. arriesgaran
23. enseñase
24. satisficiera
25. encogiese

Mastery Test 1

pp. 140–42

1. decidiré
2. estamos exigiendo
3. ellos hubieran asido
4. Juan y Pedro comieron
5. gastaríais
6. he mentido
7. ella escucha
8. estábamos viniendo
9. Uds. leyesen
10. él ha recordado
11. no caeré
12. tuvimos
13. yo hubiera pagado
14. alcancemos
15. regreso
16. él tiene

17. él no habría rezado
18. ella haya visto
19. estábamos riñendo
20. dormías
21. él caminó
22. ¿esparció ella?
23. respondisteis
24. ¿estaba Ud. sirviendo?
25. ¿correrá ella?
26. sonreímos

27. Gil, Ana y Luis asgan
28. llevaban
29. no lo creo
30. habré molido
31. ellos no convenzan
32. está lloviendo (llueve)
33. ellos vendieron
34. Ud. volvió
35. ellos se habrían vestido

Mastery Test 2

p. 142

1. I will eat
2. you might have played
3. I lie
4. we used to compete
5. he would conquer
6. you fit
7. she had convinced
8. they stumbled
9. you were preparing
10. they may deny
11. I admire
12. I have eaten
13. they will speak
14. do not decide!
15. you might have talked
16. I may maintain
17. we have said
18. you would have found

19. I washed
20. you were thinking
21. they didn't use to load
22. you had embarrassed
23. we will defy
24. I will have lit
25. you demand
26. she had supposed
27. you are lying
28. María and José will pay
29. you exercised
30. they dressed
31. we were biting
32. I would continue
33. you might indicate
34. you used to know
35. you may not stop!

Mastery Test 3

pp. 143–44

1. él se haya lavado
2. me vestí
3. nos hemos divertido
4. ella se peinó el cabello
5. ellos se lavaban
6. Uds. se han levantado
7. ellos se acordasen
8. él se estaba lavando
9. me habituaré a
10. os lavasteis
11. ella se hubiera enojado

12. ¡vistámonos!
13. me estoy acostando
14. ellos se laven
15. te habrías acordado
16. ella se está entrenando
17. él se había acostado
18. ellos se habrán esforzado
19. nos sentemos
20. ella se está enriqueciendo
21. Miguel se ha levantado
22. me irguiera

23. ellos se habituaron a
24. ella se divertía
25. me levantaré
26. ¡no os sentéis!
27. ellas se están vistiendo
28. nos graduásemos
29. ¿estamos esforzándonos?

30. Ud. se haya lavado
31. ellos se acostarían
32. me divierto
33. María se peinaba el cabello
34. él se habría entrenado
35. nos enojamos

Mastery Test 4

pp. 144–45

1. haya tomado
2. hemos medido
3. habrás desconfiado
4. ha obedecido
5. se había acostado
6. habían ejercido
7. hubiese distinguido
8. hayas dispuesto
9. hayáis influido
10. habréis sollozado
11. haya acertado
12. hubiéramos expuesto
13. habrán elegido

14. habríamos hablado
15. me he acostado
16. has subido
17. habrán aborrecido
18. habríamos movido
19. hayamos cabido
20. habéis obedecido
21. hubiesen olido
22. había elegido
23. hubiéramos corregido
24. hubiese explicado
25. ha llovido

Repaso 1

p. 145

1. he will have come
2. you smelled
3. you may say
4. Elena laughed
5. we are
6. I quarrel
7. you fitted
8. we might break the law
9. you may want
10. we are falling
11. they walked
12. he smells
13. we have conducted

14. you would have said
15. she used to wander
16. you might give
17. you deduced
18. I may have said
19. they might bless
20. I would go
21. you will have done
22. they will satisfy
23. we may go
24. you would not put
25. you might leave

Repaso 2

pp. 145–46

1. acabamos
2. habláis
3. comisteis
4. habrían partido
5. estudiarán
6. comprendan
7. hemos preguntado
8. beberéis
9. escuchaban
10. abrimos
11. entrasteis
12. vivieron
13. hubieran tomado
14. temamos
15. habremos estudiado
16. ¿se habrán graduado?
17. estábamos llevando
18. escribirían
19. comprenderemos
20. entren
21. hayan leído
22. habíamos vendido
23. habéis trabajado
24. prepararían
25. nos hubiesen amado

Repaso 3

pp. 146–47

1. yo entienda
2. hablases
3. hubiéramos dicho
4. ¡no sonrían!
5. ella hubiese desaparecido
6. yo no descubra
7. él haya dormido
8. advirtierais
9. mintamos
10. se peinase el cabello
11. Ud. haya desconfiado
12. ellos aprendan
13. hubieseis tropezado
14. yo fuera
15. ella venda
16. Ana y Juan compitiesen
17. él se vista
18. hubiéramos necesitado
19. ellos se hubieran acostado
20. Uds. no hayan torcido
21. ella recuerde
22. yo calentaría
23. hayamos enseñado
24. él siguiera
25. os hayáis levantado

Repaso 4

pp. 147–48

1. she prepares
2. are they entering?
3. we will have prevented
4. I arrived
5. you will have satisfied
6. they are mistrusting
7. we had composed
8. they would notice
9. he used to continue
10. I straighten up
11. bless us!
12. you will have analyzed
13. we might stop
14. he may conduct
15. you will sob
16. I would have fought

17. Elisa and Marta had thought
18. we might get
19. you would study
20. we will have been worth
21. they might live
22. do not lie!
23. she may impose
24. you might have persecuted
25. you were showing
26. they might go to bed
27. she mended
28. you had embraced

29. she would want
30. it will snow
31. you may have descended
32. we may live
33. he may not place
34. you used to be
35. I may have gnawed
36. you would have made
37. I compose
38. we might go
39. you might have left
40. they might get

Repaso 5

pp. 148–49

1. iré
2. está lloviendo (llueve)
3. Ud. duerma
4. habíamos lanzado
5. ellos estaban jugando
6. ella ha marcado
7. Juan y Ana supieran
8. ella habrá ejercido
9. yo conduciría
10. ¡entra!
11. hayamos dispuesto
12. ella no (se) merece
13. Uds. hubiesen encontrado

14. no vayamos
15. ellos detengan
16. él escucha
17. nos laváramos
18. yo molestaría
19. María delinquirá
20. ella vale
21. estamos viajando
22. me estoy peinando el cabello
23. influyáis
24. él había conquistado
25. ellos explicarían

Repaso 6

p. 149

A.
1. partimos
2. comíais
3. unían
4. habían salido
5. ¡acuéstense!
6. ¡no me pidáis!
7. corregiríamos
8. hayan confesado
9. se habrán acostado
10. discernieron
11. nos hubiésemos despertado
12. desapareceréis
13. bendecís
14. olamos
15. se peinaron

B.
1. marques
2. repitan
3. salgamos
4. quepa
5. consienta
6. expliquéis
7. aborrezcan
8. elija
9. hayan
10. hagan
11. vayan
12. irgamos
13. encojas
14. encuentre
15. complazca

Repaso 7

p. 150

A.

yerra, huye, cierra, gime, muere, niega, dispone, encuentra, prosigue, ha.

B.

contemos, revolvamos, castiguemos, surjamos, lavémonos, conduzcamos, parezcamos, saquemos, escondamos, santigüemos.

C.

coligiera (coligiese), mantuviese, cubriera, persiguiese, decayera, anduviese, acogiera, quisiese, durmiera, influyese.

Repaso 8

pp. 150–51

1. había acertado
2. hayan hablado
3. habrían hablado
4. habíamos dicho
5. hemos mantenido
6. habíais hecho
7. habían corrido
8. hubieras advertido
9. habré descubierto
10. habían colocado
11. hayan almorzado
12. se hubiese dispuesto
13. habéis adornado
14. me habré vestido
15. hubiéramos roído
16. habías abierto
17. he ofrecido
18. hubieran herido
19. hayáis fatigado
20. había sabido

Index of Infinitives, English to Spanish

O

obey   obedecer, 81
oblige   obligar, 73
obtain   conseguir, 77, 86
offend   ofender, 24
offer   ofrecer, 81
open   abrir, 6, 120

P

pacify   apaciguar, 74
pass   pasar, 18
pay   pagar, 72–73
persecute   perseguir, 77, 86
pity   compadecer, 81
place, put   colocar, 72; poner, 109
play   jugar, 85
please   complacer, 81
possess   poseer, 80
pray   rogar, 73, 85; rezar, 73
prepare   preparar, 18
pretend   fingir, 77
prevent   impedir, 69
produce   producir, 100
propose   proponer, 109
prosecute   proseguir, 77, 86
punish   castigar, 73
pursue   perseguir, 77, 86
put, place   poner, 109; colocar, 72

R

rain   llover, 63
read   leer, 6, 80
reach   alcanzar, 73
receive   recibir, 3, 6
recognize   reconocer, 81
reject   rechazar, 73
repeat   repetir, 69
reply   responder, 18; replicar, 72; contestar, 6
return   volver, 62, 120; devolver, 63, 120
revolve   revolver, 63, 120
risk   arriesgar, 73
run   correr, 18

S

satisfy   satisfacer, 105
say, tell   decir, 101
scatter   esparcir, 76
scratch   rascar, 72
see   ver, 119

seem   parecer, 81
seize   asir, 96; coger, 77
sell   vender, 2, 6
send   enviar, 81
serve   servir, 69
show   enseñar, 6; mostrar, 63
shrink   encoger, 77
sin   pecar, 72
sit   sentarse, 63
sleep   dormir, 66–67
smell   oler, 108
smile   sonreír, 87
snow   nevar, 63
sob   sollozar, 73
speak   hablar, 1, 8, 13, 20, 26, 31, 36–37, 42, 46, 49
spend   pasar, 18
stir   revolver, 63, 120
stop   detener, 116
study   estudiar, 6
stumble   tropezar, 73, 86
succeed   acertar, 63; conseguir, 77, 86
suppose   suponer, 109
sustain   sostener, 116

T

take   tomar, 2, 6; coger, 77
take out   sacar, 72
teach   enseñar, 6
tell   contar, 62; decir, 101
thank   agradecer, 81
think   pensar, 62
threaten   amenazar, 73
throw   echar, 18; lanzar, 73
tire   fatigar, 73
translate   traducir, 100
travel   viajar, 18
trust   confiar, 81
try hard   esforzarse, 86
turn off   apagar, 73
turnover   revolver, 63, 120

U

understand   comprender, 16; entender, 62
undertake   emprender, 24
unite   unir, 6

W

walk   andar, 96
wander   errar, 101; vagar, 73

Index of Spanish Infinitives